Praise for Other Resources from Rachel Gilmore

For *Church Programs & Celebrations for All Generations*

"At a time when churches are deluged with a variety of rehashed and recycled resources, Rachel Gilmore offers us something new. Even better, she offers something that is both practical and fun, useful and user-friendly. A great addition to the toolbox of any Christian educator." —Sam O'Neal, managing editor, SmallGroups.com for Christianity Today International

"This book is a gold mine for any pastor, educator, or youth leader who seeks to recognize Christian and secular holidays as a congregation. Each holiday becomes an event with these fresh, thorough, and insightful celebrations." —Lynn Barger Elliott, Professor of Youth Ministry, Calvin College, Youth Ministry Consultant, Youth Ministry Architects

"This book would be good for a church resource library." —*Church Libraries*, Fall 2010

"*Church Programs & Celebrations for All Generations* is a guide for making the church a cultural center . . . A must for any church leader who also wants *to be a community leader.*" —*Midwest Book Review & Library Bookwatch*, September 2010

"The activities are interactive, engaging and entertaining for everyone. The lessons have been designed for application to one's particular audience, situation, and time constraints with special emphasis on worship and fellowship. This book is a good read for anyone who is tired of watching the widening generational gap but never has had a good tool to pull it back together." —*YouthWorker Journal*, January/February 2011

"Users of this manual will appreciate the background information and other helps for leaders, and participants will benefit from the worship emphasis, appropriate scripture passages, prayers, music, and other touches such as faith station ideas and fellowship extension projects. Simple in format and without illustrations, this book will be useful for church or home educators or volunteers wishing to commemorate holidays in unique and worshipful ways." —*Congregational Libraries Today*, Issue 1, 2011

For *The Complete Leader's Guide to Christian Retreats*

"I've never seen a resource more complete and more versatile, with the basic building blocks to begin right where you are today." —from the Foreword by Jane Rubietta, conference speaker and critically acclaimed author of eleven books, including *Come Closer: A Call to Life, Love, and Breakfast on the Beach*

"Rachel Gilmore has given us an excellent how-to guide for both new and experienced retreat leaders." —William R. Myers, Director of Leadership Education (retired), The Association of Theological Schools in the United States and Canada

"This book not only gives a step-by-step guide for planning the nuts and bolts of a retreat, but it also presents eleven detailed and engaging designs for adult, youth, and family retreats that are ready to go or easily adaptable for your own group. Pastors, church educators, youth advisors, and lay leaders will especially appreciate Gilmore's conversational style and the 'need to know' tips sprinkled throughout the pages." — Nancy Jo Clendenin Dederer, Pastor, First Presbyterian Church, Homewood, Illinois

"For those who have never led a retreat AND for those who have been leaders of retreats for years, the book is a wonderful resource. Thanks for the checklists that attend to every detail." —Loretta Gratias-Bremer, Presbytery of Chicago

"Rachel Gilmore has given the gift of a handbook for 'the rest of us'—those who are not 'idea' people. *The Complete Leader's Guide* is a surefire design for a fail-proof Christian retreat—creative and biblically based." —Ellen Nolte Racheter, retired clergywoman, Christian Church (Disciples of Christ)

"I have planned and led many retreats and often wished for a book such as this." —Joyce Camp, American Baptist Women National Conference Coordinator

"Many congregations who come to your site for retreats need assistance in developing both plans and programs for their retreats. By making this book available or suggesting it to them, you can enrich their total retreat experience." —Nancy Ferguson, *RAC Newsletter* (Religiously Affiliated Camps), Winter 2008

"If you're asked to create a retreat for your church and you have no idea where to start, pick up *The Complete Leader's Guide to Christian Retreats*." —*Sojourners*, March 2009

"Rachel Gilmore has written a solid new resource for Christian retreat leaders. She covers the basics of planning and leading Christian retreats, which is very useful for persons new to retreat leadership."—Kevin Witt, Camp and Retreat Ministries, GBOD, The United Methodist Church

"Gilmore's thoroughness will allay the concerns of those who have never planned an off-site, large-group event. A priority resource for church leadership, but it's also good for a library." —*Church Libraries*, Spring 2009

"This guide will help planners and leaders avoid stress and increase enjoyment for retreat participants. Recommended for retreat planners, pastors, group leaders, camp staff, and church libraries." —*Congregational Libraries Today*, 2009

"Rachel Gilmore has provided an extensive sourcebook for anyone planning a retreat or brief 'camp' experience." —*LHP Quarterly Book Review*

JUDSON PRESS
PUBLISHERS SINCE 1824

'Tis the Season
Church Celebrations for Advent & Christmas

Rachel Gilmore

JUDSON PRESS
PUBLISHERS SINCE 1824
VALLEY FORGE, PA

'Tis the Season: Church Celebrations for Advent & Christmas
© 2011 by Judson Press, Valley Forge, PA 19482-0851

Judson Press has made every effort to trace the ownership of all quotes. In the event of a question arising from the use of a quote, we regret any error made and will be pleased to make the necessary correction in future printings and editions of this book.

Scripture quotations marked CEV are from the Contemporary English Version, copyright © 1991, 1992, 1995 by American Bible Society. Used by permission.

Scripture quotations marked MSG are from *THE MESSAGE.* Copyright © by Eugene H. Peterson 1993, 1994, 1995, 1996, 2000, 2001, 2002. Used by permission of NavPress Publishing Group.

Scripture quotations marked NIV are from the HOLY BIBLE, NEW INTERNATIONAL VERSION®. NIV®. Copyright © 1973, 1978, 1984, 2010 by Biblica, Inc.™ Used by permission. All rights reserved.

Scripture quotations marked NLT are from the *Holy Bible,* New Living Translation, copyright © 1996, 2004. Used by permission of Tyndale House Publishers, Inc., Wheaton, Illinois 60189, U.S.A. All rights reserved.

Scripture quotations marked NRSV are from the New Revised Standard Version Bible, copyright © 1989, Division of Christian Education of the National Council of the Churches of Christ in the United States of America and are used by permission. All rights reserved.

Scripture quotations marked TNIV are from the *Holy Bible, Today's New International Version®. TNIV®.* Copyright © 2002, 2004 by Biblica, Inc.™ Used by permission of Zondervan. All rights reserved.

Interior design by Beth Oberholtzer.

Cover design by Danny Ellison.

Library of Congress Cataloging-in-Publication data
Gilmore, Rachel.
    Tis the season : church celebrations for advent & christmas / Rachel Gilmore.
— 1st ed.
      p. cm.
    ISBN 978-0-8170-1697-5 (pbk. : alk. paper) 1. Advent. 2. Christmas.
3. Worship programs. I. Title.

BV40.G56 2011
263'.91—dc22

                                 2011017118

Printed in the U.S.A.
First Edition, 2011.

Contents

Appendix: Reproducible Resources and Handouts 87

Online Resources: Free Downloads and Handouts

These items can be found at www.judsonpress.com/free_ download_book_excerpts.cfm.

Introduction

It's All about the Baby—or Is It?

"In those days a decree went out from Emperor Augustus that all the world should be registered" (Luke 2:1, NRSV). I hear those words, and I am instantly transported to Christmas Eve and the balcony of my childhood church, the warmth of worshippers packed in tight, the lights turned down low for the candlelight service, and the organ tones mellow and comfortingly familiar as the notes of "What Child Is This" drift heavenward. Even from the balcony, I can smell the scent of pine boughs as I sit in my pew, reveling in the anticipation of hearing my favorite story with its proclamation: "Jesus Christ is born today."

For most of my life, Christmas was all about the baby in the manger. I remember how unsettled I felt the first Christmas in my current church when we sang not a single Christmas carol during Advent and the weekly readings for the Advent wreath had no connection to the traditional Advent themes of hope, joy, love, and peace. Instead, the scriptures crisscrossed the Old and New Testament, and the themes tied into the current message series. *How am I supposed to "prepare" for Christmas,* I wondered, *if they aren't even speaking my language?*

And the year we focused on Jesus as the Warrior King—well, I left church each week feeling radically off kilter. My theological base for Christmas was being turned upside down. Where was the story about the angel coming to Mary? And the journey to Bethlehem? And the search for an inn? And the shepherds on the hillside witnessing the revelations of the angel choir? Where was the Christmas message I knew and loved? I felt lost and confused, set adrift in the world's Christmas chaos that I'd worked so hard to avoid.

It certainly wasn't that I worshipped commercial Christmas. In fact, I'd become very anticommercial over the years, probably scarring my own three children for life as the mean mother who told them straight out that there is no Santa Claus when they otherwise would have still "believed." Spending less on stuff and giving more from the heart had become our family focus for the holidays. Yet for me, Christmas was still wrapped up in the baby.

God was continually at work in me during this time, poking holes in my assumptions. Then came the year our church did a Christmas Eve drama called *Da 3 Wise Guys* for our Christmas Eve service. A parody of all bad Italian mob comedies, *Da 3 Wise Guys* used contemporary culture references to frame their bumbling *Three Stooges*–style search for the newborn King. It wasn't that it was poorly acted; to the contrary, the actors were perfectly suited to their roles. The comic timing also hit the mark. It all worked, but for me, it was a let down. I left church feeling empty, not joyfully renewed by Christmas Eve worship. *Oh well, there's always next year,* I thought.

But apparently I wasn't the only one who couldn't relate. Two weeks later during his traditional New Year "Ask the Pastor" message, our pastor addressed the negativity that had been swirling around in the congregation since the Christmas Eve services. Speaking the truth in love, Pastor Jul said to us: "It's true. I received a lot of complaints about this year's Christmas Eve drama. People were turned off by it. They just didn't like it. They wanted to know how the holy family's journey to Bethlehem and the angels and the shepherds fit into all that pop culture stuff. Well, guess what? That drama wasn't for you. That drama was for the woman who hasn't been to church in years because it doesn't seem relevant to her life. That drama was for the man who never set foot in a church but has been looking for answers about the meaning of life and decided to visit that night. That drama was for the person who was brought up to believe that church can't be fun or funny and that God frowns on laughter and joy. So if that drama connected with just one of those people—and think of how many visitors like that we get on Christmas Eve—and made them want to know more about God's Christmas gift to the world, can you imagine how much rejoicing there was in heaven? Face it: That drama was for all the lost coins out there, not all the treasures God already has stored up in people like you. Get over it!" (Thank you, Pastor Jul, for paraphrasing liberties.)

As Pastor Jul spoke, I knew he was absolutely right, and that as much as visitors to our church needed to connect to the Christmas story through contemporary culture and comedy, I needed to get over myself and see the Christmas story through God's eyes—because it wasn't all about the baby. And it certainly wasn't all about me. When I put Jesus in that manger box, I was limiting him. Just imagine the possibilities for dynamic spiritual growth and a deeper, fuller, richer, stronger faith if I took Jesus out of that manger and let him be the man whose story started with creation and continues until the end of time!

So when my Judson Press editor, Rev. Rebecca Irwin-Diehl, approached me about creating a book of Advent and Christmas resources, I was alternately thrilled and terrified, humbled and hopeful—which I think is right where God wanted me. I was no Advent expert, being stuck for years in my conventional thinking that Christmas was all about the baby. So I researched and read and wrote and researched some more. And what I've come to proclaim without reservation is that Christmas is so much more than the baby in the box. Now that's some good news!

The goal, then, of this collection of Advent resources is to connect God's people back to God's story, from generation to generation, across the ages. It's taking the traditional Christmas stories that many people know and love and weaving them into the big picture of God's salvation plan, which didn't start with a baby born in Bethlehem but started in the birth of the world by his hand.

Unlike my second book, *Church Programs and Celebrations for All Generations*, this book doesn't have much to do with the history of the holiday, because here's the surprising thing: much of what Christians celebrate as Christmas was invented by human beings, not God. Biblical and historical scholars have debated for years over the exact birth date of Christ. It's not December 25, by the way. That date evolved in the fourth century, as the early church looked for a way to mark the birth of Christ while connecting with the pagan culture that surrounded them. Celebrating the birthday of the Light of the World on or near the winter solstice, the day that pagans celebrated the birth of the sun (the pagan light of the world) seemed to make sense. And so it stuck.

Then, by the time the Protestant Reformation took hold in the 1500–1600s, most of the high church traditions associated with wealth, formality, and legalism of the Catholic Church were frowned upon and even banned as the Protestants grew in numbers and power. For hundreds of years, Christians didn't even really celebrate Christmas, at least not with the trappings we're accustomed to now.

By the nineteenth century, however, the Victorian age of romance, culture, and civility encouraged the rebirth of Christmas carols and other sentimental traditions to mark the Savior's birth, such as evergreen garland and wreaths, decorated Christmas trees, candles, joyful singing, gift giving, feasting, and more. As the Europeans continued to migrate across the oceans, they took their customs and their faith with them, giving rise to Christian Christmas celebrations around the globe.

That's not to say that no one celebrated Christmas until the Victorian era or that Christmas symbols and traditions are of little value. However, the mission of this book is to provide opportunities for your congregation, as a family of God, together, to explore the Christmas story, which has its roots in Genesis and its happy ending in Revelation.

Here is what you'll find in these pages:

1. Overarching Advent themes of hope, love, joy, peace, light, eternal life, responsible stewardship, freedom from sin, sharing the Good News with others, and giving back to God through service to others woven throughout the eighteen programs and services.

2. A diverse selection of worship and learning formats, including informal yet reflective worship services, interactive worship services, faith and fellowship events, and dramas, geared for the entire church family.

3. A focus on hands-on, experiential learning, whether through participatory worship or faith education stations.

4. An emphasis on whole church worship and education opportunities. Intergenerational programming appeals to multiple learning styles, actively engages participants in the content, builds community across generations, and allows for both wisdom and fresh perspectives to be shared in the quest to grow in God's Word. The planning team and volunteer station hosts need to be intentional about mixing families with singles, younger members with older adults, new parents with experienced parents, and so on. Helping your congregation members learn, in the church setting, to love one another as Jesus loved us, regardless of age or faith experience, will equip them to function better out in the world and share the Good News in Jesus' name.

5. A back-to-basics approach to exploring the Bible, letting God speak through God's own Word. So often contemporary curriculum rephrases and retells what was already so perfectly authored by God, and sometimes the essence of the original story is lost in translation. Allowing worshippers and learners to hear and speak God's Word directly from Scripture takes them one step closer to writing God's Word on their hearts and being able to pass it on to all generations.

6. An understanding that all congregations are unique and a blessing. You can adapt the programs and services to fit your needs. Don't be afraid to shorten an intergenerational event by offering only one station or to substitute your own drama or favorite story into the meditation/message portion of a worship service. Especially with the fellowship portion, if you want to connect your service or program to a full meal, just plan accordingly, recruiting a kitchen and set-up crew, setting a budget and charging a fee. However, if you simply want to offer cookies and punch or not serve any refreshments at all, your planning team has that choice. Note: when planning food options, be sensitive to food allergy issues and be sure to have an ingredients list available for those who ask. Be of good courage and do what will work best for your congregation!

7. Where possible, options are given for both traditional hymns and contemporary praise and worship music. Hymns are simply listed by title; praise songs are followed by the author's name in parentheses.

8. Encouragement to dream big but start small. Do what you can with what you have this year, taking one "next step" in building up a dynamic Advent season that will transform people's hearts and minds and prepare them to celebrate Christmas from Genesis to Revelation. After Epiphany has passed, meet together to figure out your new "next step" in Advent education for the New Year and beyond.

Having taken the long and winding road to falling in love with the Christmas story that stretches from Creation to Revelation, my mission with this book is to help your congregation know that truth sooner, better, deeper, and longer. "For nothing is impossible with God" (Luke 1:37, NLT). Amen. Let it be.

PART 1

Celebrations for Worship

These seven services are designed to bring the church family together for more informal, participatory experiences in worship. They can be used as your Sunday worship service or offered as a special midweek evening or weekend afternoon option during Advent, depending on your church's needs. The services feature a mix of traditional and contemporary music, easily adapted to your church's preferences, along with interactive congregational readings and worship leadership opportunities. The Scripture passages span the Bible from Old to New Testament, with the goal of teaching the congregation that the Christmas story is not a simple, one-time event written about in Luke. It is a story that starts in Genesis and continues through the Book of Revelation and on into our lives today.

CHAPTER 1

Hanging of the Greens Worship Service

Key Verses: "Lord, you have been our dwelling place throughout all generations. Before the mountains were born or you brought forth the whole world, from everlasting to everlasting you are God" (Psalm 90:1-2, NIV).

Purpose:
a. To introduce the historical and biblical significance of Advent for Christmas
b. To connect cultural/secular Christmas traditions with faith-based traditions
c. To decorate church spaces for the Christmas season

Need-to-Know for Leaders

1. Schedule this service before the first Sunday in Advent. Note that this is an interactive service, so people will be moving and doing, as well as sitting, listening, and watching throughout worship. It is also designed as an intergenerational event that involves the entire church family, young and old alike. Do not be afraid of a little holy chaos as you come together for worship and service to prepare the way of the Lord.

2. For a smoother flow, gather all decorating materials ahead of time and arrange them in an accessible layout to facilitate the decorating process.

3. Recruit several readers, a worship leader/musician, a kitchen crew, and a setup/cleanup crew to help as needed so that the planning team can be available to oversee the decorating efforts.

Worship

What You'll Need

Note: The following list is a suggestion and can be adapted to the needs and traditions of your own church. If your church does not usually decorate extensively for Advent and Christmas, choose the decorations and aspects of the worship service that fit your congregation. For example, if you only put out an Advent wreath with candles and a Nativity scene, adapt the Order of Worship to include only the first five pieces: the Call to Worship, the Unison Prayer, the first set of four story readings (omit the Christmas tree story), the reader's response, and the sung response.

Volunteers: 2 greeters, 5 readers, worship leader/
musician, kitchen crew, setup and cleanup crew
Church Advent wreath with candles
Christmas tree(s)
Tree decorations (ornaments, garland, lights)
Extension cords
Additional garland/greens for doorways/hallways/
main worship space
Additional candles/decorative holders for worship
space
Paraments and/or Advent banners
Poinsettias
Crèche (tabletop or larger figures, indoor and/or
outdoor)
Outdoor lights and extension cords
Sticky name tags
Markers
Hymnals/song sheets/PowerPoint for song lyrics
Photocopies or PowerPoint of order of worship
Refreshments (cider/hot cocoa/coffee, Christmas
cookies, cake, etc.)
Paper goods for refreshments
PDF copies of "The Christmas Candle," "The Holly
Wreath," "The Christmas Tree," and "The Crèche"
from *Legends and Traditions of Christmas* by Trudie
West Revoir and John Pipe (rev. ed., Judson Press,
1998), online at judsonpress.com

Directions

1. Worship leader/accompanist provides a selection of Christmas music 15 minutes before scheduled start time.

2. Greeters welcome worshippers and ask them to fill out a name tag before being seated.

3. Before the service begins, the leader welcomes worshippers, explains that this is an interactive worship service, and encourages people to participate in the various activities as they are able. The leader then asks people to stand for the opening song.

Order of Worship

Opening Song: Choose one: "Come Thou Long Expected Jesus," "O Come, O Come, Emmanuel," "Majesty" (Hayford).

Call to Worship

Leader: We gather together to welcome in the season of Advent.

People: We gather together to welcome the coming of the King.

Leader: John the Baptist prepared a way in the wilderness for Jesus.

People: John cried out, "Prepare the way for the Lord, make straight paths for him" [Mark 1:3, NIV].

Leader: We cry out, "Jesus, come to us. Wonderful Counselor, Mighty God, Everlasting Father, Prince of Peace" [Isaiah 9:6, NIV].

All: We cry out, "O come, o come, Emmanuel. God is with us. We are preparing the way for you. Be with us now and always."

Unison Prayer: Lord, we come here with excitement for what lies ahead. We come here knowing that we are entering a time of busy-ness that sometimes pushes you into the background. As we prepare our church for Advent, be with us in Spirit and in Truth. Prepare our hearts and minds to know you better this Advent season, to welcome you in, to not make you wait to spend time with us this Christmas. You are the reason we are here, Lord—here on earth, and here now in this place, getting ready to celebrate your birth and the promise of your return. May each word we speak, each note we sing, each candle we light, each decoration we place remind us of your holy presence, not just in this moment, in this joyous anticipation, but in every day of our lives. May we live for you as you live for us. Amen.

Readings: "The Christmas Candle," "The Holly Wreath," "The Christmas Tree," and "The Crèche"

Reader 1: Advent is a time of waiting and preparing. One of the ways we mark the passage of days during Advent is with a wreath and candles. Each week another candle is lit to bring us closer to the celebration of Jesus' birth. Hear how early Christians used candles to remind them of the light of the world that shone into the darkness. (Read "The Christmas Candle.")

Congregational Response: Choose one: "Here I Am to Worship" (Hughes); "Silent Night," verse 3; "Shine, Jesus, Shine," verse 1 and chorus (Kendrick).

Reader 2: The greens that we use to decorate our church mean something too. Just as we'll hear in the legend of the Christmas tree, we use evergreen garland to remind us that God's love for us lives on forever. It never fades. It never dies. The holly with its red berries is a special evergreen plant with a symbolism all its own. The legend of the holly wreath is a story that has been passed on through the ages. Like other legends, it is not a story whose truth is verified by historical facts, but its truth lives in the beautiful word pictures that it paints for us, one of Jesus' never-ending love for us. Listen. (Read "The Holly Wreath.")

Congregational Response: Choose one: "The Holly and the Ivy," "Joyful, Joyful We Adore Thee," "Amazing Love" (Foote).

Note: While the congregation sings, the planning team hands out to willing volunteers the Advent wreath, the individual wreath candles, and any decorative candles/holders that will be used during Advent in the worship space and directs them on where to place the decorations. The worship leader/musicians should be prepared to continue with instrumental music after the congregational sung response if people are still placing the decorations.

Reader 3: Advent uses special colors to help us remember Jesus' birth. Originally the church used purple, which was the color of royalty and sacrifice. More recently many Protestant churches have been using blue to differentiate from the Lenten use of purple and reflect the shift by the church to celebrating God's Christmas gift to us—Jesus, the King of kings and Lord of lords. "For to us a child is born, to us a son is given, and the government will be on his shoulders. And he will be called Wonderful Counselor, Mighty God, Everlasting Father, Prince of Peace. Of the increase of his government and peace there will be no end. He will reign on David's throne and over his kingdom, establishing and upholding it with justice and righteousness from that time on and forever. The zeal of the LORD Almighty will accomplish this" [Isaiah 9:6-7, NIV].

Congregational Response: "O Come, All Ye Faithful"

Note: While the congregation is singing, the planning team hands paraments and/or banners to willing volunteers and assists them in placing them on the lecterns, communion table, walls, etc. The worship leader/musicians should have additional instrumental music prepared as needed.

Reader 4: The tradition of having Christmas trees in homes started in Europe and was brought to the United States in the early 1800s. Even for Americans who don't focus on Jesus' birth as the reason to celebrate Christmas, the Christmas tree connects them to the idea of everlasting life through the evergreen tree. Listen to the story of how the little fir tree became a part of traditional Christmas celebrations. (Read "The Christmas Tree.")

Congregational Response: Choose one: "O Christmas Tree," "Deck the Halls," "Hark! The Herald Angels Sing."

Reader 5: Christian families often display a nativity scene as part of their traditional decorations on a tabletop or outdoors. Seeing the holy family, the shepherds, the stable animals, the angels, and even the magi gathered around the infant King helps us remember that this season of Advent is not all about us. It helps us remember God's story, our story, the story of the greatest gift ever given. Listen now to the legend of the crèche. (Read "The Crèche.")

Congregational Response: Choose one: "Away in a Manger," "Infant Holy, Infant Lowly," "This Is Our God" (Tomlin).

Note: While the congregation sings, the planning team should hand pieces of a tabletop nativity set to be placed on display in front. If you need to move the display to another location after worship, volunteers can do that as well.

The Charge

Leader: *(Modify to fit your situation.)* People of God, we are now going to move out and fully prepare this place for Advent so that we might honor the baby Jesus, as well as the grown Jesus who has promised to return to us in glory. After we sing the next song, you may choose where you want to work: decorating the worship space, setting up a large nativity scene outside, or decorating the church Christmas tree(s). We will work for about an hour. As your group finishes, please join us for refreshments in the fellowship hall. Amen!

Congregational Response: Choose one: "Children, Go Where I Send Thee," "Here I Am, Lord," "Joy to the World."

Note: A planning team member should be assigned to each work group to provide instructions for where decorations are to be placed and to keep participants on task.

Fellowship

1. The kitchen crew should have refreshments ready for participants as they filter in after their work time.

2. The suggested menu includes: hot cider/hot cocoa/ coffee, Christmas cookies, cake, pretzels, snack mix, etc.

3. Additional options include playing Christmas music or running an animated Christmas DVD for smaller guests who may be done with structured program time.

4. Fellowship is open-ended, and participants may leave whenever they are ready.

CHAPTER 2

Re-Creation: An Advent Drama and Worship Service

Need-to-Know for Leaders

1. This service can be used during Advent or on Christmas Eve to provide an overview of our God-history. It incorporates a short drama that uses middle and high school youth actors.

2. The planning team should schedule at least two or three rehearsals before the service to practice the drama. If your church is new to drama, you may want to begin practices in October or early November so that your cast and crew have plenty of time to feel comfortable in their roles.

3. If possible, use middle and high school youth as musicians and vocalists.

4. This service can be shortened by choosing only one song in each of the congregational singing parts and by omitting the unison prayer.

What You'll Need

Volunteers: greeters, worship leader/musician(s)/vocalist(s), director and/or drama assistants, drama cast (6 actors, see script that follows), lighting tech

Photocopies of song sheets, hymnals, or PowerPoint with lyrics

Photocopies of scripts for participants

Advent wreath with candles

Matches or lighter

Optional but very helpful: wireless handheld, lavaliere, or head-set microphones for speaking characters

Key Verse: "Those who have been born into God's family do not make a practice of sinning, because God's life is in them. So they can't keep on sinning, because they are children of God" (1 John 3:9, NLT).

Purpose:
a. To involve teenagers in presenting the good news of Christmas
b. To connect the Creation story to the Christmas story
c. To turn people's hearts and minds to Jesus as they turn away from sin

Directions

1. Greeters should seat worshippers and provide an Order or Worship, if using one.

2. Provide 10–15 minutes of music before the service, using a youth band, MP3 player, or CDs with worship songs/hymns/carols selected by the youth.

3. Worship leader/musicians should welcome worshippers and open the service with a time of singing, followed immediately by the drama.

Order of Worship

Meditative Music

Opening Songs: Choose three or four. Suggestions include "Unfailing Love" (Tomlin), "Glory in the Highest" (Tomlin), "Favor of the Lord" (Houghton), "Doxology" (Crowder), "O Praise Him" (Crowder).

Drama: *Re-Creation* (See script at right or online at www.judsonpress.com.)

Unison Prayer: We, the people, in order to form a more perfect union with the Holy One, acknowledge our failings, our brokenness, our mistakes, our pride, our false wisdom—to put it simply, our sin. We lay it all down at the feet of the baby in the manger, at the feet of the man on the cross. Holy, holy, holy are you Lord, God of power and might. Heaven and earth are surrounded, infused, energized, renewed by your glory. In spite of us, because of us, because of your ultimately selfless, self-sacrificing gift of your son to us, we have life, and have it abundantly. Praise God! For this gift, planned from the dawn of Creation, offered freely and continuously to the dawn of the new heaven and new earth, we give you thanks, O Lord, our God. Joy to the world! The Lord is come!

Sung Response: Choose two or three choruses. Suggestions include "Create in Me a Clean Heart" (Green), "Give Us Clean Hands" (Hall), "Thank You for Hearing Me" (original lyrics by Sinead O'Connor, adapted by David Crowder Band).

Benediction

Leader: People of God, know that Jesus is the Alpha and the Omega, the beginning and the end of all life. Leave this place renewed, restored, and ready to make a difference in his kingdom. Go in peace. Go with God.

Talk Back (Optional)

If your team is willing, consider offering a Talk Back session after the service. Allow the congregation to ask questions of cast, crew, and director(s) to further process the drama's message and its potential impact on people for the remainder of Advent and beyond.

Re-Creation
by Rev. Keith Hesselink*

Setting: Garden of Eden

Scenery/props: a tree of life mural or potted tree, an apple, Advent wreath with candles (3 blue tapers, 1 pink taper; white center pillar), matches or lighter, recording of Apologetics's "You Booked It All Along," recording of Jeremy Camp's "I Am Nothing," recording of Dave Matthews Band's "The Maker"

Costumes: Adam and Eve, green t-shirts; Readers, everyday clothing; Serpent, dull gray or camouflage pants and shirt; Angel, fancy/shiny clothing or tunic (gold, silver, red, purple, etc.), optional tinsel halo

Cast:

Adam	Reader 2
Eve	Serpent
Reader 1	Angel

Tech note: Lighting fades to black for opening of drama. "You Booked It All Along" by Apologetics (verse 1 only) starts playing quietly then grows louder as the lights come up on stage. Keep the congregation in the dark with spotlights on each reader if possible. Music fades out before Reader 1 begins. Reader 1 stands on far left of stage; Reader 2 stands on far right of stage. Adam and Eve are in center back by tree of life. Serpent is offstage to begin. The Advent wreath is front and center with a taper lighter or matches easily accessible.

Reader 1: God said, "Let us make human beings in our own image, to be like us. They will reign over the fish in the sea, the birds in the sky, the livestock, all the wild animals on the earth, and the small animals that scurry along the ground." So God created human beings in his own image. In the image of God he created

*Adapted by Rachel Gilmore. Used with permission.

them; male and female he created them. Then God blessed them and said, "Be fruitful and multiply. Fill the earth and govern it. Reign over the fish in the sea, the birds in the sky, and all the animals that scurry along the ground" [Genesis 1:26-28, NLT].

Tech note: Spotlight moves to Reader 2.

Reader 2: This is the account of the creation of the heavens and the earth. When the LORD God made the earth and the heavens, neither wild plants nor grains were growing on the earth. For the LORD God had not yet sent rain to water the earth, and there were no people to cultivate the soil. Instead, springs came up from the ground and watered all the land. Then the LORD God formed the man from the dust of the ground. He breathed the breath of life into the man's nostrils, and the man became a living person.

Then the LORD God planted a garden in Eden in the east, and there he placed the man he had made. The LORD God made all sorts of trees grow up from the ground—trees that were beautiful and that produced delicious fruit. In the middle of the garden he placed the tree of life and the tree of the knowledge of good and evil [Genesis 2:4-9, NLT].

Tech note: Spotlight moves to Adam, who has moved to front center stage position. Eve is still behind him by the tree of life.

Adam: Oh man, I don't know how to describe it accurately enough to you. Everything "in the beginning" was so beautiful. It was all fresh and brand-new. I sat with the Maker, and we looked at all of creation. God always told me it was good. But it was better than good. It was utterly awesome! The colors of the trees were bright and bold. They were so fresh with life. They grew so quickly, so straight and sturdy. I spent a good amount of time every day trimming them and picking their fruit. The fruit was so plump and juicy. Even the vegetables were great. Everything tasted so gooood. Every bite was like a little piece of heaven. I tried them all—apples, pears, figs, pomegranates, tomatoes, cucumbers, and brussels sprouts. Yes, in the Garden of Eden even brussels sprouts tasted *great*! Everything was deee-licious. I ate all of the fruits and vegetables—except of course the ones the Maker told me not to touch.

One day the Maker came by with a bunch of animals. I had no idea what they all were. I guess God didn't either, since it was *my* job to give them all names. It took a while because there were so many of them. I'm glad I got the Creator's creative mind, or it would have been impossible to think up so many different names. Which do you think is more creative—the word *platypus* or the animal itself?

You really should have been there. The place was so incredibly bright!

Tech note: Adam moves to Advent wreath and lights four candles as Reader 1 continues. Spotlight moves to Reader 1 as Adam stays by wreath while Reader 1 continues.

Reader 1: The LORD God placed the man in the Garden of Eden to tend and watch over it. But the LORD God warned him, "You may freely eat the fruit of every tree in the garden—except the tree of the knowledge of good and evil. If you eat its fruit, you are sure to die."

Then the LORD God said, "It is not good for the man to be alone. I will make a helper who is just right for him." So the LORD God formed from the ground all the wild animals and all the birds of the sky. He brought them to the man to see what he would call them, and the man chose a name for each one. He gave names to all the livestock, all the birds of the sky, and all the wild animals. But still there was no helper just right for him.

So the LORD God caused the man to fall into a deep sleep. While the man slept, the LORD God took out one of the man's ribs and closed up the opening. Then the LORD God made a woman from the rib, and he brought her to the man [Genesis 2:15-22, NLT].

Tech note: Spotlight moves back to Adam.

Adam: I was thankful for all the gifts the Maker gave to me, life born of the divine image, a garden to tend, fish, birds, animals roaming around the place. And the Maker said that *I* was in charge of them. Imagine, all that beauty God had made, and he let *me* be in charge. All the Maker asked was for me not to eat from one of the many trees. Seemed reasonable. That's another gift the Maker gave me—free will, choice. God could have easily made it impossible for me to even get at that tree, but it was right there in the garden with everything else the Maker had made, which meant I had the choice to obey or not. Amazing! Oh, and the Maker gave me a partner. It was getting a little lonely there, so God made me a partner—made out of me. Took one little bone out of me, added some dirt, some God-breath, and there she was! Someone to share my life with, someone to share in my responsibilities. What a God! Life was so good!

Tech note: Spotlight moves to Reader 2.

Reader 2: Now the serpent was the shrewdest of all the wild animals the LORD God had made. One day he asked the woman, "Did God really say you must not eat the fruit from any of the trees in the garden?"

"Of course we may eat fruit from the trees in the garden," the woman replied. "It's only the fruit from the tree in the middle of the garden that we are not allowed to eat. God said, 'You must not eat it or even touch it; if you do, you will die.'"

"You won't die!" the serpent replied to the woman. "God knows that your eyes will be opened as soon as you eat it, and you will be like God, knowing both good and evil" (Genesis 3:1-5 NLT).

Tech note: Spotlight moves to Serpent at center stage.

Serpent: Those two thought the Maker was so cool. They did everything he asked them to do. I just didn't get it. So the Maker created some life. Big deal! All-powerful—what about me? Well, I could be powerful, too. So I decided to do something about it. I figured the one weakness the Maker left open was that silly gift of free will. I would never have done that. You want complete control over your servants, you make them prisoners—make them puppets. Hollow obedience is still obedience. Besides, it is really about control, not love and obedience, right?

So that's where I attacked. The Maker had told them not to eat from the tree of the knowledge of good and evil or they would die. What's so bad about knowing about good and evil? If I did it right, they wouldn't think it was such a big deal either. Their Maker had that knowledge, so why shouldn't they have it too? Why not be like the Maker? If you ask me, the reason they weren't allowed to eat from it was because then the Maker wouldn't be so special. *"Hey, you won't die; you'll be more like your Maker."* That's *what I'll tell them,* I thought.

It was a pretty good plan. *Oh, and I think I'll hit on the woman first,* I told myself. *The man was told by the Maker himself not to eat that fruit—the guy might be more resistant. He might not go for it as fast. But the woman—she was probably told by the man not to do it—so I'll start a little wedge between them. She might think, "He can't tell me what to do."* Besides, directions never seem as strict when they come secondhand. Look at how tempting that is—sweet luscious fruit, ultimate knowledge. "Here, just try a little," I'd say. "It will taste sooo gooood!"

Tech note: Serpent goes to Advent wreath and snuffs out four candles with glee as Reader 1 continues. Serpent then goes to stand by the tree of life next to Eve. Spotlight shifts to Reader 1.

Reader 1: The woman was convinced. She saw that the tree was beautiful and its fruit looked delicious, and she wanted the wisdom it would give her. So she took some of the fruit and ate it. Then she gave some to her husband, who was with her, and he ate it, too. At that moment their eyes were opened, and they suddenly felt shame at their nakedness. So they sewed fig leaves together to cover themselves.

When the cool evening breezes were blowing, the man and his wife heard the LORD God walking about in the garden. So they hid from the LORD God among the trees. Then the LORD God called to the man, "Where are you?"

He replied, "I heard you walking in the garden, so I hid. I was afraid because I was naked."

"Who told you that you were naked?" the LORD God asked. "Have you eaten from the tree whose fruit I commanded you not to eat?"

The man replied, "It was the woman you gave me who gave me the fruit, and I ate it."

Then the LORD God asked the woman, "What have you done?"

"The serpent deceived me," she replied. "That's why I ate it."

Then the LORD God said to the serpent, "Because you have done this, you are cursed more than all animals, domestic and wild. You will crawl on your belly, groveling in the dust as long as you live. And I will cause hostility between you and the woman, and between your offspring and her offspring. He will strike your head, and you will strike his heel" [Genesis 3:6-15].

Tech note: Serpent steps forward to front center stage. Spotlight moves to Serpent.

Serpent: Ha, she fell for it! I'm so brilliant and devious! And she got the man to do it too. Use the one against the other. I can use that tactic over and over and over again. And I will strike their heels so many times they won't know what's happening. And that crush my head stuff—how are these puny little people going to be able to crush me? I just tricked them with a piece of fruit. Unless . . . I wonder: could the Maker have meant something else? Naw, God wouldn't do that—right? Could be a nasty battle brewing. . . .

Tech note: Serpent returns to position by Eve and the tree. Spotlight moves to Reader 2.

Reader 2: Then God said to the woman, "I will sharpen the pain of your pregnancy, and in pain you will give birth. And you will desire to control your husband, but he will rule over you."

And to the man he said, "Since you listened to your wife and ate from the tree whose fruit I commanded you not to eat, the ground is cursed because of you. All your life you will struggle to scratch a living from it."

Then the man—Adam—named his wife Eve, because she would be the mother of all who live [Genesis 3:16-17,20, NLT].

Tech note: Eve moves forward to front center stage. Spotlight moves to Eve.

Eve: I really regret it now. That dirty little serpent got the best of me, poisoning me against my Maker. Why would I even listen? I was content with life with Adam and all that the Maker had given us. There was only that one simple little rule about one certain tree. That is until that serpent made me question why some fruit was forbidden. It slithered up to me and got me to forget about all that we were given and then focus on the one thing I couldn't have. How stupid of me! But at that moment, that snake in the grass pushed me to the edge, and I jumped.

Temptation—I hate that word. I knew what the Maker had said, but when the serpent spit out those words, they were, well, a lot louder than the Maker's words. Somehow I felt that I needed to eat from *that* tree. I needed to be more like the Maker. It *sounded* like a worthy goal. So I took a bite! That's when it all fell apart. That dirty serpent grinned—a grin that sent shivers down my back.

I should have talked it over with Adam before I took it. Although he sure didn't hesitate very long when I offered it to him, so . . . maybe it wouldn't have mattered. Either way, the damage was done. And the consequences—not good! The Maker kicked us out of the garden. The land outside the garden didn't seem to produce food as good as when we were inside. And the soil was much, much harder for Adam to cultivate. He worked his tail off every day to feed our family, a family that soon grew bigger. And then I realized another consequence of our action. The Maker said childbirth would be more painful. Painful does not describe it. Cain was a thirteen-pound baby! Talk about pain.

I do sense now, though, that another baby may play a part in all of this someday!

Tech note: Eve goes and lights the Christ candle. Spotlight moves to Reader 1.

Reader 1: "And I will cause hostility between you and the woman, and between your offspring and her offspring. He will strike your head, and you will strike his heel" [Genesis 3:6-15].

Tech note: Spotlight moves to focus on Eve, who appears to be weeping and wrestling with the consequences of her actions while "I Am Nothing" by Jeremy Camp plays. If Eve is also a singer, she could sing this as a solo instead. As the song ends, Eve walks over to Adam and they move off to the side of the stage and sit or kneel on the floor, far away from the tree of life. Then spotlight moves to Reader 2.

Reader 2: Then the LORD God said, "Look, the human beings have become like us, knowing both good and evil. What if they reach out, take fruit from the tree of life, and eat it? Then they will live forever!" So the LORD God banished them from the Garden of Eden, and he sent Adam out to cultivate the ground from which he had been made. After sending them out, the LORD God stationed mighty cherubim to the east of the Garden of Eden. And he placed a flaming sword that flashed back and forth to guard the way to the tree of life [Genesis 3:22-24, NLT].

Tech note: Spotlight moves to Angel who is standing at front center stage.

Angel: Unbelievable. *Un-be-lieve-able!* They had paradise . . . and tossed it away! We couldn't believe it. Oh, excuse me, I should introduce myself. I'm one of the cherubim placed at the entrance to Eden, the one with a flaming sword. We cherubim are a type of angel, but that's another message for another time.

Anyway, like I said, we couldn't believe these two tossed it all away. After the whole serpent thing, we figured the Maker would just zap Adam and Eve and start the whole thing over again. You know—leave the earth to the animals and do the human thing over again on maybe . . . oh, say, Riegil 7. But no! The Maker wanted to save them, salvage the whole project. Amazing! It would have been a whole lot easier to just start all over, we thought. Yet we really should have known better.

The Maker has these bizarre concepts that always work out. It's amazing, really! I mean, who knew? Thinking back, we should have known something was up when the Maker mentioned the "crushing the head and striking the heel" thing. But come on, the reality of it was, creation was trashed. Nevertheless, the Maker was determined to re-create the whole thing—the dirt, the plants, the animals . . . and the people. The method the Maker chose was also really bizarre, but you'll be hearing more about that in the next few weeks I imagine.

But I digress. My role at Eden was to guard the entrance so those two wouldn't eat fruit off of the other tree—the tree of life. Can't even imagine how horrible that scenario would have been. A bunch of totally corrupt people living forever?

But again, as it turned out, that is what the Maker had in mind. The Maker chose to restore creation, and to do it by *re*-creating it. Of course the process this whole re-creation thing took was rather messy. Like Noah and that flood incident. Can you say *soggy*? The mess with Moses and those people in Egypt—very sloppy. We kinda thought that David with his kingdom stuff was on to something, but look how that turned out . . . bust! And then Bethlehem . . . Wow! Wow! Wow!

There is a lot more to the re-creation story, but I can let you in on the ending. When the baby Savior comes back to see you, not as a baby of course, but as the Judge, just know that everything, *everything*, will be made right again, and the whole creation will rejoice with the Maker.

Tech note: Angel relights all four candles while "The Maker" by the Dave Matthews Band plays and lights fade to black, leaving only candlelight. Angel and Readers 1 and 2 move to the tree of life and stand to its left while Serpent stands to the right of the tree.

CHAPTER 3

Living Out Loud: An Interactive Worship Service

Key Verse: John replied in the words of Isaiah the prophet, "I am the voice of one calling in the wilderness, 'Make straight the way for the Lord'" (John 1:23, NIV).

Purpose:

a. To actively involve the congregation in the Christmas story

b. To introduce/reintroduce "classic" Advent/Christmas texts (Isaiah's prophecy, Mary's song of praise, the journey to Bethlehem, the shepherds and the angels)

c. To send worshippers out into the world with a firm foundation of the Christian definition of Christmas

Need-to-Know for Leaders

1. This service is interactive in design, so be prepared for things not to flow perfectly. The point is to help people actively engage in God's Word by becoming part of the story using the biblical texts that weave together to form the Christmas narrative. Simple costumes and encouragement from your drama assistants will facilitate congregational participation.

2. Volunteers of all ages can be used for the speaking parts during the service, but they need to be able to read. Some nonspeaking parts are available as well.

3. Isaiah should be played by an older youth or adult, because he needs to read by candlelight for a few moments.

4. The eight sung responses and three additional songs in the Order of Worship were specifically chosen for their thematic connection to each preceding passage of Scripture or prayer, as well as their representing a diversity of music from contemporary praise choruses to hymns, from Christmas carol to African traditional, crossing both denominations and generations.

5. Consider preparing the giveaway candy cane Christmas cards ("Advent"ure 7 in chapter 15, page 74) for worshippers to take on their way out to share with friends, neighbors, and coworkers. The planning team may want to add "www.rethinkingchristmas.org" to the cards to encourage people to shift the focus of Christmas away from material things and back to the things of God.

6. In addition, the team may choose to film the service and post it on YouTube and/or your church website to spread God's Word in one more way.

7. This service can be shortened by omitting Interactive Readings 5 and 8, as well as the Preparation for Prayer music and Sung Response after the prayer.

What You'll Need

Volunteers: worship leader/musician(s)/vocalist(s), narrator, 3–5 drama assistants, lighting tech

Participant readers recruited before the service for Isaiah, John the Baptist, Mary, Elizabeth, Gabriel, Angels, and King Herod

Participant actors (no lines) recruited before the service for Joseph, 3 innkeepers, shepherds, 3 magi, star carrier

Simple Bible-time costumes: robe/belts for Mary, Joseph, Elizabeth, Isaiah; fur tunic for John the Baptist; 3 gifts and 3 crowns for 3 magi; crown for King Herod; shepherds' crooks; tinsel garland crowns for angels; small pillows for pregnant Mary and Elizabeth

Props: doll wrapped in blanket; manger; 2 chairs; 2' gold star mounted on a 3–4' pole with gold ribbons hanging down

Photocopies of song sheets, hymnals, or PowerPoint with lyrics

Photocopies of interactive reading scripts for participants are available online at www.judsonpress.com

Poster-size cue cards with verbal/nonverbal cues for congregation (could also put these into PowerPoint)

Optional: candy cane Christmas card giveaways (See chapter 15, page 74 for directions.)

Optional: videographer and video camera/tripod

Optional but very helpful: wireless handheld or headset microphones for readers

Directions

1. Ask the worship leader/musicians/vocalists to provide meditative background music beginning 15 minutes before the service.

2. Ask the drama assistants to welcome worshippers and recruit people to play Isaiah, John the Baptist, Mary, Elizabeth, Gabriel, Joseph, Joseph's angel, the innkeepers, the shepherds, the shepherds' angels, King Herod, and the three magi. Those who agree will be told when to come forward and will be given a simple costume and a cue card with a few lines. Encourage both children and adults to take on these roles.

3. Drama assistants should divide up the cast and be responsible for assisting their characters with their lines and movements throughout the service.

Order of Worship

Meditative Music

Interactive Reading 1: Isaiah 9:2-7 (See script.)

Sung Response: "Jesus, Name above All Names" (Hearn)

Interactive Reading 2: Mark 1:1-8 (See script.)

Sung Response: "Freedom Is Coming" (African traditional)

Interactive Reading 3: Luke 1:26-38 (See script.)

Sung Response: "Take My Life" (hymn version, verse 1, or contemporary by Underwood)

Interactive Reading 4: Luke 1:39-56 (See script.)

Sung Response: "Be Thou My Vision," verse 1

Interactive Reading 5: Matthew 1:18-25 (See script.)

Sung Response: "Here I Am, Lord," verse 1

Interactive Reading 6: Luke 2:1-7 (See script.)

Sung Response: "O Little Town of Bethlehem," verse 1

Interactive Reading 7: Luke 2:8-20 (See script.)

Sung Response: "Hark! the Herald Angels Sing," verse 1

Interactive Reading 8: Matthew 2:1-12 (See script.)

Sung Response: "We Three Kings of Orient Are," verse 1

Preparation for Prayer: "Create in Me a Clean Heart" (Green)

Unison Prayer: Lord, we come before you now, filled with a sense of awe and wonder for your story, our story. Help us to keep this awe and wonder in our hearts as we go back out into the world, a world filled with pressure, a world filled with pain, a world filled with too much, a world filled with not enough. Yet you are there, as you always have been, as you always will be. We fall on our knees like the magi and pray that your love, your presence, will continue to guide us like the star of Bethlehem. Help us to live your story out loud, not just here in this place, but out in your world where your Word can make a difference if we pass it along. We lift up to you now, Lord, prayers for ourselves—for strength, for confidence, for courage, for patience, for second chances when we turn away and forget your story—and prayers for others, Lord, for those who need healing, for those who need wholeness, for those who need a second chance. Be in our lives. Be in their lives. Help us to be at work in this world in your name, Lord. Amen.

Sung Response: "Of the Father's Love Begotten"

Benediction

Leader: People of God, know this: God loved you so much that he sent his only Son to this broken, battered world to live and die for us, so that whoever knows him, loves him, and serves him will never die but live with him forever in God's heavenly house. Go be lights in this world and shine for God. Live your life out loud and share the good news of Christmas: Glory to God in the highest, and on earth, peace, goodwill to all people who seek to know the Lord.

Closing Song: "Joy to the World"

Scripts

Note: Drama assistants and the narrator should have a master copy of all scripts. For each interactive reading, the assistants should give the readers/actors costumes (if needed), scripts, and microphones (if available) and position them according to the script directions. The assistants should continue to cue the participants as needed and seat them when their section is complete. Nonspeaking characters can be prompted by the drama assistants. Assistants can use multiple poster-size cue cards to cue the congregation for additional movements/phrases. Use the sung responses to transition the speakers/actors to and from their seats.

Isaiah Script / Interactive Reading (IR) 1

* Scripture references in order: Isaiah 9:2-4; 9:6-7, NLT

Tech note: Bring lights all the way down. After Isaiah lights the candle, gradually bring the lights back up to a low level that allows people to read the cue cards. Isaiah needs a robe with belt and a candle and lighter or matches.

Narrator: *(will need to have these opening lines memorized or use a penlight)* The prophet Isaiah ministered to God's people almost 750 years before Jesus' birth. One of the things he talked to them about was the fact that a Savior would be born who would rescue them

once and for all from their sins. God's people then, just as now, had a hard time staying on track and following God's Word. Life was hard, and the world offered a lot of alternatives to God's truth. Yet Isaiah spoke into that brokenness and proclaimed that life changes were coming. Listen to what he said:

Isaiah: *(kneeling, head bowed, facing away from the congregation and toward cross or altar; lights a candle and begins speaking while kneeling; worship area lights gradually come up to reading levels)* The people who walk in darkness will see a great light. For those who live in a land of deep darkness a light will shine. You [O God] will enlarge the nation of Israel, and its people will rejoice. They will rejoice before you as people rejoice at the harvest and like warriors dividing the plunder. For you will break the yoke of their slavery and lift the heavy burden from their shoulders. You will break the oppressor's rod, just as you did when you destroyed the army of Midian [who fought against Gideon and his small number of men].*

(Isaiah rises and faces congregation, speaks more loudly.) For a child is born to us, a son is given to us. The government will rest on his shoulders. And he will be called:

(For each of the following, assistants show the congregation poster-size cue cards or PowerPoint slides with the text.)

Isaiah and Congregation Group A: Wonderful Counselor.

Isaiah and Congregation Group B: Mighty God.

Isaiah and Group A: Everlasting Father.

Isaiah and Group B: Prince of Peace.

Isaiah: His government and its peace will never end. He will rule with fairness and justice from the throne of his ancestor David for all eternity. The passionate commitment of the LORD of Heaven's Armies will make this happen!*

Tech note: Fade to black.

John the Baptist Script / IR 2

* Scripture references in order: Mark 1:2-3; 1:3; 1:7-8, NLT

Tech note: Bring lights up to normal reading level. John needs a fur tunic.

Narrator: About seven hundred years after the end of Isaiah's ministry, John the Baptist entered the picture, a fellow servant of the Lord who fulfilled another of Isaiah's prophecies. Isaiah had given God's people this information: "Look, I am sending my messenger ahead of you, and he will prepare your way. He is a voice shouting in the wilderness."*

John the Baptist: Prepare the way for the Lord's coming! Clear the road for him.*

Narrator: John was kind of an odd guy, but he was a guy who knew his place in life. His only job was to get the people ready to meet his cousin Jesus, who was not yet working in ministry. Jesus was still working as a carpenter with his father Joseph. So John hung out by the Jordan River, wearing camel skin and eating locusts and honey, and he spoke God's Word to God's people.

John the Baptist: Someone is coming soon who is greater than I am—so much greater that I'm not even worthy to stoop down like a slave and untie the straps of his sandals. I baptize you with water, but he will baptize you with the Holy Spirit!*

Mary/Gabriel/Elizabeth Script / IR 3 & 4

* Scripture references in order: Luke 1:28; 1:30-33; 1:26-37; 1:42-45; 1:46-50; 1:51-55, NLT

Tech note: Lights should be a little lower from the John the Baptist levels. If possible, light stage area one half at a time to focus first on Mary and Gabriel and then on Mary and Elizabeth. Mary and Elizabeth each need a robe/belt. Gabriel needs a tinsel garland crown. For added effect, place a pillow under Elizabeth's robe to show her pregnant form.

Narrator: Going back in time again, we meet Mary, a Jewish teen from a humble, hardworking family living in Nazareth. Mary was engaged to Joseph, a carpenter, also a Jew from a humble, hardworking family. Both families could trace their ancestors back to King David. Mary was going about her daily life, making plans for her wedding and starting her new life with Joseph, when God suddenly and miraculously interrupted her plans, sending his angel Gabriel to talk with Mary.

Gabriel: Greetings, favored woman! The Lord is with you!*

Narrator: Mary was confused by the angel's words and wondered what they meant. Then the angel told Mary:

Gabriel: Don't be afraid, Mary, for you have found favor with God! You will conceive and give birth to a son, and you will name him Jesus. He will be very great and will be called the Son of the Most High. The Lord God will give him the throne of his ancestor David. And he will reign over Israel forever; his Kingdom will never end!*

Mary: *(to Gabriel)* How can this happen? I am not married!

Gabriel: The Holy Spirit will come upon you, and the power of the Most High will overshadow you. So the baby to be born will be holy, and he will be called the Son of God. What's more, your relative Elizabeth has become pregnant in her old age! People used to say she was barren, but she's now in her sixth month. For nothing is impossible with God.*

Tech note: Switch lighting to other half of stage area if possible. Gabriel may be seated back in the congregation. As the narrator begins speaking, Mary moves to sit/stand on the other half of the stage with Elizabeth. Assistants will need poster-size cue cards for the congregation for the end of the Luke passage. (The remainder of this script is IR 4.)

Narrator: A few days later, Mary hurried to the hill country of Judea, to the town where Zechariah (and Elizabeth) lived. She entered the house and greeted Elizabeth. At the sound of Mary's greeting *(Mary hugs Elizabeth; Elizabeth places her hand on her belly and exclaims, "Oh!")*, Elizabeth's child leaped within her, and Elizabeth was filled with the Holy Spirit.

Elizabeth: God has blessed you above all women, and your child is blessed. Why am I so honored, that the mother of my Lord should visit me? When I heard your greeting, the baby in my womb jumped for joy. You are blessed because you believed that the Lord would do what he said.*

Mary: Oh, how my soul praises the Lord. How my spirit rejoices in God my Savior! For he took notice of his lowly servant girl, and from now on all generations will call me blessed. For the Mighty One has done great things for me. He shows mercy from generation to generation to all who fear him.*

(Again, assistants will use poster-size cue cards or PowerPoint slides for the following text.)

Mary and Congregation Group A: His mighty arm has done tremendous things! He has scattered the proud and haughty ones.

Mary and Group B: He has brought down princes from their thrones and exalted the humble.

Mary and Group A: He has filled the hungry with good things and sent the rich away with empty hands.

Mary and Group B: He has helped his servant Israel and remembered to be merciful.

Mary and Groups A and B: For he made this promise to our ancestors, to Abraham and his children forever.*

Joseph/Angel Script / IR 5

* Scripture references in order: Matthew 1:20-21; 1:18-25, NLT

Tech note: Keep the lighting fairly low for the nighttime meeting of Joseph and the angel. Joseph should lie down on the stage. The angel should stand over him. Mary should be seated off to the side of the stage, head bowed. Joseph should wear a robe/belt. The angel can wear a tinsel garland crown.

Narrator: Well, when Joseph found out that his bride to be was pregnant, he didn't know what to do. According to Jewish law, engaged women who became pregnant by another man were to be stoned to death. Joseph loved Mary; he didn't want her to die from that awful punishment. He was planning to just quietly send her away and readjust his own plans for his future. But once again, God suddenly and miraculously interrupted Joseph.

Angel: I appeared to Joseph in a dream and I said, "Joseph, son of David, do not be afraid to take Mary as your wife. For the child within her was conceived by the Holy Spirit. And she will have a son, and you are to name him Jesus, for he will save his people from their sins."*

Narrator: All of this occurred to fulfill the Lord's message through the prophet Isaiah: "Look! The virgin will conceive a child! She will give birth to a son, and they will call him Immanuel, which means 'God is with us.'" When Joseph woke up *(Joseph stands and moves to take Mary's hand)*, he did as the angel of the Lord commanded and took Mary as his wife.*

Tech note: Bring lighting back up to reading level for sung response.

Mary/Joseph/Innkeepers Script / IR 6

* Scripture references: Luke 2:1-7, NLT

Tech note: Lighting can stay at normal reading levels. Actors may wear biblical costumes if desired. For added effect, Mary can place a pillow under her robe for her walk to Bethlehem. Position several innkeepers throughout the worship area where Mary and Joseph can approach each one in turn, seeking shelter. Position last innkeeper up front on stage. Set up a manger and two chairs on the opposite side of the stage from the last innkeeper. Place a doll wrapped in a blanket in the manger. Mary and Joseph may sit there for the remainder of the vignettes.

(As the narrator speaks, Mary and Joseph travel through the worship area, approaching the innkeepers, pantomiming the need for a place to stay. Innkeepers shake their heads no and wave them on.)

Narrator: At that time the Roman emperor, Augustus, decreed that a census should be taken throughout the Roman Empire. (This was the first census taken when Quirinius was governor of Syria.) All returned to their own ancestral towns to register for this census. And because Joseph was a descendant of King David, he had to go to Bethlehem in Judea, David's ancient home. He traveled there from the village of Nazareth in Galilee. He took with him Mary, his fiancée, who was now obviously pregnant. *(Pause and wait for couple to approach stage innkeeper and be seated.)* And while they were there, the time came for her baby to be born. She gave birth to her first child, a son. She wrapped him snugly in strips of cloth and laid him in a manger, because there was no room for them in the village inn.*

Mary/Joseph/Shepherds/Angels Script / IR 7

*Scripture references in order: Luke 2:8-9; 2:10-12; 2:14; 2:15-20, NLT

Tech note: Lower lighting to almost darkness to indicate nighttime visit to the shepherds. Mary and Joseph remain seated up front. Mary now has baby in her arms. A few shepherds who come to the manger may carry crooks. Lead angel may wear a tinsel garland crown. Congregation Group A will be the mass of shepherds on the hillside and will follow the nonverbal cue card directions. Group B will be the angel choir and read the verbal cue card lines.

Narrator: That night there were shepherds staying in the fields nearby, guarding their flocks of sheep. Suddenly, an angel of the Lord appeared among them, and the radiance of the Lord's glory surrounded them. *(Bring up lights to full power.)* They were terrified.* *(Assistants show cue card that reads "shake and moan in fear, hold hands up over eyes" to Group A and have them tremble and hide from the light. Assistants can encourage them verbally if needed.)*

Angel: *(speaking to shepherds)* Don't be afraid! I bring you good news that will bring great joy to all people. The Savior—yes, the Messiah, the Lord—has been born today in Bethlehem, the city of David! And you will recognize him by this sign: You will find a baby wrapped snugly in strips of cloth, lying in a manger.*

Angel and Congregation Group B: *(Assistants show verbal cue card to Group B that reads)* Glory to God in the highest heaven, and peace on earth to those with whom God is pleased.*

Narrator: When the angels had returned to heaven, the shepherds said to each other, "Let's go to Bethlehem! Let's see this thing that has happened, which the Lord has told us about." *(Two to four congregational shepherds move forward to Mary and Joseph on stage and kneel down before manger.)* They hurried to the village and found Mary and Joseph. And there was the baby, lying in the manger. After seeing him, the shepherds told everyone what had happened and what the angel had said to them about this child. All who heard the shepherds' story were astonished, but Mary kept all these things in her heart and thought about them often. The shepherds went back to their flocks, glorifying and praising God for all they had heard and seen. It was just as the angel had told them.*

King Herod/Magi/Star Carrier Script / IR 8

*Scripture references in order: Matthew 2:8; 2:9-12, NLT

Tech note: Keep lighting at minimal reading levels. The magi need regal costumes (but no crowns) and props that represent the gifts of gold, frankincense, and myrrh. King Herod needs a crown. Mary and Joseph remain seated up front. The star carrier needs the star on the pole.

Narrator: *(Assistants direct star carrier to proceed up to stage and stand between Herod and holy family. Magi leave their seats in congregation, follow the star, and approach stage where King Herod stands opposite Mary and Joseph.)* Time has passed, probably almost two years. Mary and Joseph have stayed in Bethlehem, but life is getting dangerous. Three magi from the East have arrived in Jerusalem asking about the baby born to be King of the Jews. For King Herod, the current earthly king, this spells trouble. Herod does a little research and then tells the magi:

Herod: *(speaking to three magi)* Go to Bethlehem and search carefully for the child. And when you find him, come back and tell me so that I can go and worship him, too!*

Narrator: Of course, this was not really his plan. His secret, evil plan was to kill this baby king and to let the magi lead him right to Jesus. Well, the magi went on their way. *(Assistants direct star carrier to move behind holy family and hold star high above baby's head. Magi follow star carrier, kneel down in front of manger, and present gifts to family.)* And the star they had seen in the east guided them to Bethlehem. It went ahead of them and stopped over the place where the child was. When they saw the star, they were filled with joy! They entered the house and saw the child with his mother, Mary, and they bowed down and worshiped him. Then they opened their treasure chests and gave him gifts of gold, frankincense, and myrrh. When it was time to leave, they returned to their own country by another route, for God had warned them in a dream not to return to Herod.*

(Magi leave worship area by a side aisle and return to their seats.)

CHAPTER 4

An Advent Service of Hope

Leader Need-to-Know

1. Children are most welcome to be a part of this service because they are part of the church family and because they, too, experience illness, loss, sadness. The story that is shared during the service is kid-friendly and hopeful, but parents should be made aware of the potential for this service to be a little more emotionally intense. People may cry, but children can learn that the family of God comes together to comfort one another and remind each other of the hope we have in Jesus. If your congregation has a wide spread of ages and you expect a large number of very young children, the planning team may wish to have a children's room set up with child care available.

2. Be sure to choose a date for this service the week before or the week that Advent begins to provide the greatest benefit for worshippers who are struggling with grief and loss during the holidays.

3. Consider also running a grief support class like Grief Share (www.griefshare.org) during Advent that could start on the following day or week or offering a short-term small group using a book such as *On the Road to Emmaus* by Myrlene Hamilton Hess (Judson Press, 2008).

4. Publicize your service or class ahead of time in the local papers, on your church website, and through your regular publicity avenues.

Key Verses: "Why am I discouraged? Why is my heart so sad? I will put my hope in God! I will praise him again—my Savior and my God!" (Psalm 42:5-6, NLT).

Purpose:
a. To allow the faith community to grieve for what is lost: loved ones, friendships, relationships with Jesus, health, happiness, wholeness, and so on.
b. To take comfort in the unity of the Spirit present in worship and reaffirmed through God's Word
c. To offer healing and hope in Jesus' name to those who experience the Christmas season as a time of hopelessness and sadness

What You'll Need

Volunteers: prayer teams (volunteers who will pray
  for and with worshippers at designated locations),
  story reader, greeters, worship leader/musician(s)/
  vocalist(s)

Slips of paper

Pens

Collection basket for prayer concerns

Shiny new pennies

Photocopies or PowerPoint of order of worship

Drawing paper and crayons for children for meditation

Tape

Boxes of facial tissues for prayer stations

Directions

1. Set up the worship space so that participants have access to a group seating area with plenty of room to spread out if they desire personal space. An area should be reserved for prayer teams, either scattered in quiet corners or perhaps on your chancel if not using a full choir. Provide seating for the prayer team and the worshippers. Place a box of tissues nearby each prayer station.

2. Play meditative music in the worship area at least 20 minutes ahead of service time.

3. Greeters should welcome worshippers and offer an order of worship, along with several sheets of drawing paper and crayons to children. Let families know the drawing paper will be used by the children during the meditation.

4. Greeters should also invite worshippers to write down on the slips of paper the names of friends/loved ones who have died or are ill or other prayer concerns that are weighing on them. These will be shared during the service. Collect slips in a basket before worshippers enter.

Order of Worship

Meditative Music

Call to Worship: (Psalm 122, CEV, adapted)

Leader: It made me glad to hear them say, "Let's go
     to the house of the LORD!"

People: Jerusalem, we are standing inside your gates.

Leader: Jerusalem, what a strong and beautiful city
     you are!

People: Every tribe of the LORD obeys him and comes
     to you to praise his name.

Leader: David's royal throne is here where justice
     rules.

People: Jerusalem, we pray that you will have peace,
     and that all will go well for those who love you.

Leader: May there be peace inside your city walls
     and in your palaces.

People: Because of my friends and my relatives, I will
     pray for peace.

Leader: And because of the house of the LORD our
     God, I will work for your good.

People: We come to worship you, O God. Our feet
     are standing at your gates.

Leader: The lost, the lonely, the hurt, the spiritually
     hungry—we all come before you, Lord, seek-
     ing help, seeking hope. Hear our prayers,
     Lord, spoken and unspoken, as we lift up to
     you those things that make us feel lost and
     without hope.

Worship leader allows a time of silent prayer and closes this time by lifting up the names/concerns written on the slips of paper. Leader asks worshippers to respond to each name/concern with the phrase "Lord, we put our hope in you."

All: Let us seek God together and worship him in
     Spirit and in truth. Amen.

Assurance of Pardon

Leader: We gather before God, wearing our masks, hiding our shame, denying our pain, ignoring our need for wholeness. We want to be part of this festive time, to celebrate the birth of Christ, to be joyful with friends and family, to look forward toward the start of a new year. Yet often we can't. We feel stuck in the miry clay of lost hope that pulls us down and holds us in the pit of our despair, our worry, our anxiety. None of us is immune. All of us, at times, assume we are alone. But hear the good news: As a community of faith, we can come together, we can bear one another's burdens, and we can receive the assurance of forgiveness that God graciously gives to all of his children because of the sacrifice of his Son. In fact, hear these reassuring words from Jesus' Sermon on the Mount of Olives in the book of

Matthew: "God blesses those who are poor and realize their need for him, for the Kingdom of Heaven is theirs. God blesses those who mourn, for they will be comforted. God blesses those who are humble, for they will inherit the whole earth. God blesses those who hunger and thirst for justice, for they will be satisfied. God blesses those who are merciful, for they will be shown mercy. God blesses those whose hearts are pure, for they will see God. God blesses those who work for peace, for they will be called the children of God. God blesses those who are persecuted for doing right, for the Kingdom of Heaven is theirs" (Matthew 5:3-10, NLT). And this is our hope, that although we daily fight against the ways of the world and we covet security and a sense of belonging, when we say we are children of God, we are blessed. As members of the family of God, there is always room for one more when we seek to live by his Word. Receive that gift of hope, that there is room for you in the family of God. Amen.

Note: Leader can substitute the other New Testament readings according to the lectionary year if desired.

Sung Response: Choose a song your congregation knows well. Suggestions include "Amazing Grace," "I Want Jesus to Walk with Me," "Come Thou Fount," "Come Ye Disconsolate" (Moore), "My Life Is in You, Lord" (Gardener), "Grace Like Rain" (Agnew), "Let the Redeemed" (Barnett) or "I'm Trading My Sorrows" (Evans).

Meditation: "Room for One More"

The reader should preface the story with the following:

Our hope is in Jesus, who was and is and is to come. His birth was the first coming. He will return again to gather up his believers. We do not know the hour. We simply trust in God to make good on his promise. Until that time, we wait, we watch, and we hope, using every opportunity given to turn away from our sins, to lay down our burdens and draw near to Jesus. There is always room for one more in the household of God. Listen to the following parable about belonging.

Reader asks children to take out their drawing paper and crayons and draw pictures that go along with the story as he or she reads the story (see appendix, pages 89–90) and when finished says:

Let us now bring our fears, worries, imperfections, hurts, pain, and sadness to the Lord. Take this time to give these things to Jesus and let him give you his comfort, his assurance of hope, in return. You are welcome to pray where you are at, to gather with your family and friends and pray quietly together, or to move to one of the prayer stations and have our prayer teams pray for and with you. Let us come to God in prayer. Children, please bring your pictures forward during this time, and we will hang them around the worship space.

Play meditative music and allow people to have time to pray silently, in small groups, or with prayer teams (about 5 minutes). The speaker or planning team members can help the children hang their drawings in the worship space, encouraging them to stay quiet and whisper during the prayer time. This may feel long, so the planning team will need to monitor how people are doing and whether people are waiting in lines at the prayer team stations. Ask the worship leader to prepare additional music in order to accommodate your congregation's needs.

Offering

Leader: Tonight we are doing a reverse offering. The offering baskets coming your way are filled with shiny new pennies. Please take one out as it passes by you. Hold it in your hand. Put it in your pocket. Carry it with you this Advent. Let it remind you of Jesus' story of the lost coin. Jesus spoke of a woman who lost a single coin and looked everywhere for it, frantic to find it, hoping against hope that it would appear. And when she found it, she rejoiced. Jesus says that all of heaven rejoices jubilantly like that over lost souls who have been found. Do you feel like that lost coin, hidden away in the dark, unable to see the light? Hold that penny and know that Jesus is searching for you always, ready to release you from your hurt, from your fear, and from your pain no matter how far away and how hidden you feel. Hold on to that hope.

Offering Song: "O Come, O Come, Emmanuel"

Benediction

Leader: Hear these words from the prophet Isaiah: "The Spirit of the Sovereign LORD is on me, because the LORD has anointed me to proclaim good news to the poor. He has sent me to bind up the broken-hearted, to proclaim freedom for the captives and release from darkness for the prisoners, to proclaim the year of the LORD's favor and the day of vengeance of our God, to comfort all who mourn" (Isaiah 61:1-2, NIV). Go in peace. Go in hope and know that there is room for you in the family of God. For those who would like to remain for meditation and reflection, the worship area/sanctuary will stay open for an additional hour. Our prayer teams will also stay for those who would like to meet with them. Go in peace and live in hope. Amen.

Continue to have meditative music playing and allow those who need more time to stay and pray silently or move to the prayer teams.

CHAPTER 5

An Advent Service of Love

Need-to-Know for Leaders

1. Children are most welcome to be a part of this service since they are part of the church family, but this service has a lengthy responsive reading, as well as a more adult-focused meditation on Mother Teresa and her service to God. It will depend on your church's customs, but the planning team may want to set up a childcare room for children kindergarten-age and younger, although parents may opt to keep infants with them in the service. The total service will run 40–45 minutes, so a Christmas video and some art supplies should keep most little ones busy. Another option would be to substitute a different, child-friendly reading for the meditation, like Maurice Sendak's *Where the Wild Things Are*, Shel Silverstein's *The Giving Tree*, Margaret Wise Brown's *The Runaway Bunny*, or another story about the power of love.

2. This service marks the second week of Advent with its theme of love and related Advent lectionary readings, so schedule accordingly.

3. Don't forget to publicize your service and/or class ahead of time in the local papers, on your church website, and through your regular publicity avenues.

Key Verse: "Love and faithfulness meet together; righteousness and peace kiss each other" (Psalm 85:10, NIV).

Purpose:
a. To emphasize the gift of love that God gave the world
b. To equip worshippers to prepare the way for God's gift of love to enter the world
c. To send worshippers out into the world to love one another as Jesus loved us

What You'll Need

Volunteers: worship leader/musician(s)/vocalist(s), greeters, 4 readers

John the Baptist costume (fur tunic, beard, walking stick, sandals, etc.)

Photocopies or PowerPoint of order of worship

Photocopies of song sheets, hymnals, or PowerPoint with lyrics

Advent wreath with candles

Matches or lighter

PDF copy of pages 66–70 about Mother Teresa from *Crazy Faith* by Susan K. Williams Smith (Judson Press, 2009), available at www.judsonpress.com

Boxes of tissues for prayer stations

Optional: drawing paper or 8' length of mural paper and crayons

Directions

1. Ask the worship leader/musicians/vocalists to provide meditative background music beginning 15 minutes before the service.

2. Ask greeters to welcome worshippers, offer an order of worship if using photocopies, and invite them to be seated and enjoy a time of quiet meditation before the service begins.

Order of Worship

Meditative Music

Choral Call to Worship: Worship leader welcomes worshippers, invites them to stand, and then moves the congregation from one song into the next using spoken or instrumental transitions. Suggested songs—any combination of three or four songs, depending on your congregation's needs/traditions: "Jesus Loves Me," "Jesus Loves the Little Children," "Come to Jesus," "Lord, I Want to Be a Christian," "Love Divine, All Loves Excelling," "What Wondrous Love Is This?," "Love Came Down on Christmas," "It Came upon the Midnight Clear" (verses 1, 3, 5), "Love, Love," "Blessed Be Your Name" (Redman), "Come, Now Is the Time to Worship" (Doerksen), "How Deep the Father's Love for Us" (Townend), "More Love, More Power" (Jude Del Hierro), "Your Grace Is Enough" (Tomlin).

Responsive Reading: Taken from Isaiah 40:1-11 and Mark 1:1-8 (NLT). Use 2 readers up front and 1 reader in back who should be dressed like John the Baptist. He will speak his first lines from the back and then move down the center aisle to the front, so in larger sanctuaries and where the technology is available, use a wireless headset microphone.

Reader 1: "Comfort, comfort my people," says your God. "Speak tenderly to Jerusalem. Tell her that her sad days are gone and her sins are pardoned. Yes, the LORD has punished her twice over for all her sins."

Reader 2: Listen! It's the voice of someone shouting,

John: Clear the way through the wilderness for the LORD! Make a straight highway through the wasteland for our God! Fill in the valleys, and level the mountains and hills. Straighten the curves, and smooth out the rough places. Then the glory of the LORD will be revealed, and all people will see it together.

Reader 2: The Lord has spoken!

Reader 1: A voice said, "Shout!"

Reader 2: I asked, "What should I shout?"

Reader 1: Shout that people are like the grass. Their beauty fades as quickly as the flowers in a field. The grass withers and the flowers fade beneath the breath of the LORD. And so it is with people. The grass withers and the flowers fade. . .

All: ". . . but the word of our God stands forever."

Reader 2: O Zion, messenger of good news, shout from the mountaintops!

All: The word of our God stands forever.

Reader 1: Shout it louder, O Jerusalem. Shout, and do not be afraid. Tell the towns of Judah, "Your God is coming!"

All: The word of our God stands forever.

Reader 2: Yes, the Sovereign Lord is coming in power. He will rule with a powerful arm. See, he brings his reward with him as he comes.

All: The word of our God stands forever.

Reader 1: He will feed his flock like a shepherd. He will carry the lambs in his arms, holding them close to his heart. He will gently lead the mother sheep with their young.

All: The word of our God stands forever.

Reader 1: This is the Good News about Jesus the Messiah, the Son of God. It began just as the prophet Isaiah had written: "Look, I am sending my messenger ahead of you, and he will prepare your way. He is a voice shouting in the wilderness . . ."

John: *(moving down the center aisle toward front)* Prepare the way for the Lord's coming! Clear the road for him!

All: The word of our God stands forever.

Reader 2: *(reads while John continues to move to the front and faces congregation)* This messenger was John the Baptist. He was in the wilderness and preached that people should be baptized to show that they had repented of their sins and turned to God to be forgiven. All of Judea, including all the people of Jerusalem, went out to see and hear John. And when they confessed their sins, he baptized them in the Jordan River. His clothes were woven from coarse camel hair, and he wore a leather belt around his waist. For food he ate locusts and wild honey. John announced:

John: Someone is coming soon who is greater than I am—so much greater that I'm not even worthy to stoop down like a slave and untie the straps of his sandals. I baptize you with water, but he will baptize you with the Holy Spirit!

All: The word of our God stands forever. Thank you, God, for the gift of your Son, the gift of love that never ends, the promise of salvation that bears all things, believes all things, hopes all things, endures all things. The word of our God stands forever. Amen!

Note: Leader can substitute the other New Testament readings according to the lectionary year if desired.

Sung Response: Choose one: "Away in a Manger" (verses 1, 3), "What Child Is This?" (verses 3, 4, 5), "Silent Night" (verse 3).

Meditation: Reading from *Crazy Faith* by Susan K. Williams Smith, pages 66–70.

Note: If your church uses PowerPoint, you may want to find photos of Mother Teresa engaged in her life's work and show them on the screen during the reading.

The reader should preface the story with the following:

Love came down at Christmas. This love offering from God to us was not given to be passively accepted but joyfully used. So often we forget that God gave us this love first because he so loved us, and he desperately wants us to share that love with others. When we work purposefully on pouring out God's love on the world, we begin to make straight the roads in the wilderness and prepare the way for Jesus to return to us again. One woman who came to understand that and live a life of love was Mother Teresa. Listen to a little bit of her story and how she decided to live a life of love. *(Reader reads excerpt.)*

After reading the excerpt, the reader should close with these words:

What a woman, what a God, don't you think? How are you making a way in the wilderness for Jesus? Are you preparing the way for him? Are you loving him with joyful,

thankful hearts? Are you serving him to the best of your ability? Psalm 85:8-13 (CEV) says: "I will listen to you, LORD God, because you promise peace to those who are faithful and no longer foolish. You are ready to rescue everyone who worships you, so that you will live with us in all of your glory. Love and loyalty will come together; goodness and peace will unite. Loyalty will sprout from the ground; justice will look down from the sky above. Our LORD, you will bless us; our land will produce wonderful crops. Justice will march in front, making a path for you to follow." Consider the path that you are following. Consider the path that you are preparing for those who follow you.

Let's go to God in prayer and ask for wisdom and faithful obedience in preparing a path for him in this world, because the "word of our God stands forever," and we want to send that word out into the world.

Silent Prayer: Play meditative music for approximately 5 minutes to allow people to pray silently. This may feel long, so the planning team will need to monitor how people are doing and if more or less quiet time is desired. Have additional music ready and adjust according to your congregation's needs. The team may also want to have individual sheets of drawing paper or an 8' length of mural paper available and invite children to come forward during the prayer time to draw their prayers.

Sung Response: Choose one: "Prayer of St. Francis," "Precious Lord, Take My Hand," "Give Us Clean Hands" (Hall).

Benediction

Leader: Hear these words from the book of John: "In the beginning the Word already existed. The Word was with God, and the Word was God. He existed in the beginning with God. God created everything through him, and nothing was created except through him. The Word gave life to everything that was created, and his life brought light to everyone. . . . So the Word became human and made his home among us. He was full of unfailing love and faithfulness" (John 1:1-5,14, NLT). Go out into the world in love. Make straight paths for the King who is coming again, full of unfailing love and faithfulness.

All: The word of our God stands forever. Amen!

Closing Song: "O Come, All Ye Faithful" or "Sing to the King" (Foote)

CHAPTER 6

An Advent Service of Joy

Need-to-Know for Leaders

1. Children are most welcome to be a part of this service since they are part of the church family, but there is quite a bit of choral reading involved in this service. The planning team may wish to set up a childcare room for children ages 5 or 6 and younger, although parents may choose to keep infants with them in the service. Total service length should run about 40–45 minutes, so a Christmas video and some art supplies should keep little ones busy.

2. This service marks the third week of Advent with its theme of joy and related Advent lectionary readings, so schedule accordingly.

3. Don't forget to publicize your service ahead of time in the local papers, on your church website, and through your regular publicity avenues.

4. To further enhance the joyful nature of this worship service, the planning team may opt to decorate the worship space with additional pink candles (traditionally a pink candle, called the rose candle, is used in an Advent wreath to mark the third week), pink banners, or pink streamers/ribbons on the pews/chairs.

5. The planning team has the option of inviting the children forward during the prayer time to draw their prayers on an 8' length of mural paper or on individual sheets.

Key Verse: "How my spirit rejoices in God my Savior!" (Luke 1:47, NLT).

Purpose:
a. To help worshippers focus on joy that comes from God, not from stuff
b. To share joys and concerns of the congregation through multiple prayer opportunities (sung, silent, spoken, group, individual, etc.)
c. To celebrate the joy of Advent through music (sung and instrumental)

What You'll Need

Volunteers: worship leader/musician(s)/vocalist(s), greeters, 3 readers/leaders

Bible-time costumes for Isaiah (robe with rope belt, sandals), Mary (robe with belt, sandals, head covering), and a psalmist (robe with rope belt, sandals, guitar or small lyre)

Photocopies or PowerPoint of order of worship

Photocopies of song sheets, hymnals, or PowerPoint with lyrics

Advent wreath with candles

Matches or lighter

Additional pink candles/streamers/banners for decoration

Small (2"–3") pink hearts

Pens

Collection basket

PDF copy of pages 16–18 about John Tigrett's Decision from *Modeling Mary in Christian Discipleship* by John Burns (Judson Press, 2007), available at www.judsonpress.com

Optional: 8' length of mural paper or individual sheets of drawing paper and crayons

Directions

1. Ask the worship leader/musicians/vocalists to provide meditative background music beginning 15 minutes before the service.

2. Ask greeters to welcome worshippers and offer an order of worship if using photocopies.

3. Greeters should also invite worshippers to write down any joys or concerns they have on the pink hearts. These can be placed in a basket outside the worship area and brought in to be shared during the service.

4. During the service, worshippers will participate in a choral reading. Three readers/leaders dressed as Mary, Isaiah, and a psalmist will each be responsible for leading one-third of the congregation in reading their passages out loud. The text will need to be written out on the order of worship or done in PowerPoint. The following sample service uses the New Living Translation for all verses. Your planning team can choose whatever version best speaks to your congregation.

Order of Worship

Meditative Music

Call to Worship

Leader: This is the day that the Lord has made!

People: Let us rejoice and be glad in it!

Choral Call to Worship: Planning team/worship leader can choose any combination of two or three songs to prepare the congregation to celebrate our joy in the Lord. Possibilities include "O Come, All Ye Faithful," "Good Christian Friends, Rejoice" (verses 1 and 2), "Joyful, Joyful, We Adore Thee," "This Is My Father's World," "How Great Is Our God" (Tomlin), "Trading My Sorrows" (Evans).

Unison Prayer: Wonderful Counselor! Mighty God! Everlasting Father! Prince of Peace! We come to you, filled with excitement and anticipation of the Christmas season, but also filled with the excess of the Christmas season—the pressure, the guilt, the nonstop commitments, the need to exceed, the need to live large. Rein us in, Lord. And then once you've got us in your grip, we beg of you, Lord, reign in us. Have your way in us. Joy is found in you, Lord. True joy comes from knowing and trusting that you will provide for all our needs, that you will fix our broken places, that you will bind up our broken hearts, that you will set us free from the worldly things that hold us prisoner. As we seek you now in worship, calm us, still us, slow us down, let us breathe—that we might be filled with your Spirit, that we might overflow with your joy. Amen.

Contemporary Costumes?

Think about Mary as a teenage mother and dress her in leggings or jeans and an oversized t-shirt. Isaiah might resemble a modern-day preacher in a power suit. The psalmist might look like a struggling musician with holey jeans and a rock band t-shirt. Get creative and ask your actors to brainstorm their own costumes.

Choral Reading: Taken from Isaiah 61:1-3,8-11; Luke 1:47-55; and Psalm 126 (NLT). Use 3 readers up front dressed in costume to each lead one-third of the congregation in their part.

Psalmist: Let us speak together God's word and revisit the joy of our faith-filled ancestors, the saints who have gone before us. Listen to how, across the generations of God's people, God's word echoes with the same truth, the same joy.

Psalmist and Psalmist's Choir: When the LORD brought back his exiles to Jerusalem, it was like a dream! We were filled with laughter, and we sang for joy. And the other nations said, "What amazing things the LORD has done for them." Yes, the LORD has done amazing things for us! What joy!

Mary: And I sang out to the Lord:

Mary and Mary's Choir: How my spirit rejoices in God my Savior! For he took notice of his lowly servant girl, and from now on all generations will call me blessed. For the Mighty One is holy, and he has done great things for me.

Isaiah and Isaiah's Choir: I am overwhelmed with joy in the LORD my God! The Spirit of the Sovereign LORD is upon me, for the LORD has anointed me to bring good news to the poor. He has sent me to comfort the brokenhearted and to proclaim that captives will be released and prisoners will be freed. He has sent me to tell those who mourn that the time of the LORD's favor has come.

Sung Response: Choose one or two songs. Possibilities include "Hark! the Herald Angels Sing," "My Soul Gives Glory to My God," "It Is Well with My Soul," "There Is Joy in the Lord" (Keaggy).

Choral Reading: Continue as above.

Psalmist and Psalmist's Choir: Restore our fortunes, LORD, as streams renew the desert. Those who plant in tears will harvest with shouts of joy. They weep as they go to plant their seed, but they sing as they return with the harvest.

Mary and Mary's Choir: He shows mercy from generation to generation to all who fear him. His mighty arm has done tremendous things! He has scattered the proud and haughty ones. He has brought down princes from their thrones and exalted the humble. He has filled the hungry with good things and sent the rich away with empty hands.

Isaiah and Isaiah's Choir: And the Lord said, "For I, the LORD, love justice. I hate robbery and wrongdoing. I will faithfully reward my people for their suffering and make an everlasting covenant with them."

Sung Response: Choose one or two songs. Possibilities include "It Came upon the Midnight Clear," "I Am Thine," "Trees of the Field" (Rubin and Dauermann), "Humble Thyself" (Hudson), "I Exalt Thee" (Sanchez).

Choral Reading: Continue as above.

Mary and Mary's Choir: He has helped his servant Israel and remembered to be merciful. For he made this promise to our ancestors, to Abraham and his children forever.

Isaiah and Isaiah's Choir: And the LORD said, "Their descendants will be recognized and honored among the nations. Everyone will realize that they are a people the LORD has blessed." The Sovereign LORD will show his justice to the nations of the world. Everyone will praise him! His righteousness will be like a garden in early spring, with plants springing up everywhere.

Sung Response: Choose one or two songs. Possibilities include "Jesu, Joy of Man's Desiring," "Joy to the World," "God Is Great" (Zschech).

Meditation: Reading from *Modeling Mary in Christian Discipleship* by John Burns, pages 16–18, or other joy-inspiring meditation of your choice.

Note: If your church uses PowerPoint, you may want to find various illustrations of Mary as she is transformed from lowly servant status to a woman who can say, "All generations will call me blessed," and show them on the screen during the reading.

The reader should preface the excerpt with the following:

"What are mere mortals that you should think about them, human beings that you should care for them?" (Psalm 8:4, NLT). Yet God does think of us. God has always been thinking of us, caring for us, hoping against hope that we will return the love he so freely offered and offers in the gift of his Son. That gift alone should bring us joy, and yet we are so human, caught up in our own mortality, our own materialism, that we forget to look at what a life with God offers—true, Spirit-filled joy. Listen to a different perspective now on Mary's story and consider why she chose a life of joy.

After reading the excerpt, the reader should close with these words:

Like Timothy, like Samuel, like Jeremiah and other young believers, Mary offers us an example of true discipleship, of living with joy in the midst of a life overwhelmed with concern, of living for God in a world set against him. As we come to God in prayer and share the joys and concerns on our hearts, let's also consider how we might set aside worldly joy and accept God's divine delight instead.

Musicians should play meditative music for approximately 5 minutes to allow people to pray silently. Children can be invited forward to draw their prayers on the mural paper or on individual sheets. The reader/leader can close out prayer time by sharing the joys and concerns left in the collection basket and then inviting the congregation to pray these words from 1 Thessalonians 5:16-22 (NLT) aloud:

Lord, let us always be joyful. Help us never to stop praying and to be thankful in all circumstances, for this is your will for us. Guard us against stifling the Holy Spirit or scoffing at prophecies, but give us the wisdom to test everything that is said. May we always hold on to what is good and stay away from every kind of evil. These things we pray in your Son's precious name. Amen.

Closing Song: "Go Tell It on the Mountain"

Benediction

Leader: Hear these words of Paul to the people of Thessalonica: "Now may the God of peace make you holy in every way, and may your whole spirit and soul and body be kept blameless until our Lord Jesus Christ comes again. God will make this happen, for he who calls you is faithful" [1 Thessalonians 5:23-24, NLT]. Go out into the world in joy and serve your God with unbridled passion so that all generations will look at you and call you blessed.

All: "How my spirit rejoices in God my Savior!" [Luke 1:47, NLT]. Amen!

CHAPTER 7

An Advent Service of Peace

Key Verse: "Your unfailing love will last forever. Your faithfulness is as enduring as the heavens" (Psalm 89:2, NLT).

Purpose:

a. To provide a quiet time and breathing space for worshippers during "Christmas craziness"

b. To encourage worshippers to lay down their burdens and accept Jesus' gift of spiritual peace

c. To prepare worshippers to go out and share God's peace with the world

Leader Need-to-Know

1. Children are welcome to be a part of this service as they are part of the church family, too. However, of the four Advent services in chapters 4 through 7, the peace service is the most meditative. While it's good for children to see worshippers modeling quiet time and to experience quiet time themselves, the 15-minute chunks may be hard for younger children. The planning team should publicize the more meditative nature of this service, note that older children are welcome and encouraged to fully participate, but also provide a childcare option for second graders and under. Total service length will again run approximately 45 minutes. If the planning team expects grade-school youth to attend the service, they might want to encourage participants to bring pillows or blankets to spread on the floor during the quiet and guided meditation times, if your church has the space for this. In addition, the childcare team may want to offer an activity where they read the Luke or Colossians passage from the service and then play quiet, meditative music while the children draw their prayers or thoughts about God in response.

2. This service marks the fourth and final week of Advent with its theme of peace and related Advent lectionary readings, so schedule accordingly.

3. Don't forget to publicize your service ahead of time in the local papers, on your church website, and through your regular publicity avenues.

What You'll Need

Volunteers: worship leader/musician(s)/vocalist(s), greeters, 1 reader/leader, 2 meditation station hosts

Photocopies or PowerPoint of order of worship

Photocopies of song sheets, hymnals, or PowerPoint with lyrics

Advent wreath with candles

Matches or lighter

Small (3"–4") paper peace symbols, 1 per person (find a reproducible graphic online by searching for "peace symbol" or trace jar lids and draw a thick Y in their center, then copy)

Pens

A 3'-6' cross for Meditation Station 1

Price tags (one per person, 3" x 5" index cards with corners clipped on one short side and a center hole punched on that end) to hang on the cross, preprinted with the meditation verse citation (Luke 1:26-38; computer-generated and printed on self-stick address labels)

6" sections of yarn to tie price tags to cross

Bibles for both meditation stations

Religious Christmas cards in sealed envelopes (one per person) with verse citation printed in each one (Colossians 3:12-17; use computer-generated self-stick address labels)

Photocopies of the "next steps" directions for each meditation station

PDF copy of Psalm 23 guided meditation, pages 41–43, from *The Complete Leader's Guide to Christian Retreats* by Rachel Gilmore (Judson Press, 2008), available at www.judsonpress.com

Directions

1. Ask the worship leader/musicians/vocalists to provide background meditative music beginning 15 minutes before the service.

2. Ask greeters to welcome worshippers and offer an order of worship if using photocopies.

3. Greeters should also invite worshippers to take one paper peace symbol and a pen with them into worship. Adults should assist children as needed with the writing activity in this service.

4. During the service, worshippers will be invited to move to two different meditation spaces where there will be an opportunity for them to read and reflect on a Scripture passage and then write a "next step" on the peace symbol.

5. Meditation spaces may be done in either order.

6. For worshippers wishing to remain seated, the primary reader/leader can bring those people a price tag and a Christmas card so they can complete the meditation activities in their seats.

7. The worship leader can give the general instructions to the congregation before beginning this portion of the service so that people understand the flow, saying: *In a moment you can move to either meditation space and take a price tag or card. Find and read the Bible verses printed on the tag or card, and then reflect on those words and how they might direct your "next step" in finding God's peace. Take a moment to write down your "next step" on your peace symbol. Then move to other meditation space when you are ready, and return to your seats when cued by the worship leader.*

8. For the first meditation space, decorate an area in the worship space with advertising flyers representing "commercial Christmas"—the hokier and more obnoxious the better. Consider adding light-up decorations or other items that will emphasize the pressure to join the world's Christmas craziness.

- Also in this space, place a cross (can be any shape/form you wish) with the preprinted price tags hanging from it. The host at this station can invite people to take a price tag, read and reflect on it in relation to the "next step" directions, and then write their "next step" on one side of their peace symbol.

- The "next step" directions for this meditation space read as follows: *Read Luke 1:26-38 and consider Mary's dilemma. Her once organized, acceptable marriage plans got turned upside down by Gabriel's message. How did Mary respond to her own version of Christmas craziness? What is a "next step" you can take to find a bit of peace in the world's Christmas craziness? Write that "next step" on one side of your peace symbol.*

9. For the other meditation space, lay out a variety of religious Christmas cards in envelopes. The cards should have preprinted in them Colossians 3:12-17 (printed on self-adhesive labels). The station host should invite people to take a card, find and read the passage, reflect on it in relation to the "next step" directions, and then write their individual "next step" on one side of their peace symbol.

- The "next step" directions for this meditation space read as follows: *Read Colossians 3:12-17. As you work to let the peace of Christ rule your heart, how can you also share that peace of God that passes all understanding? Think about a "next step" you can take to pass on God's peace to someone this Christmas season.*

Order of Worship

Meditative Music

Call to Worship

Leader: God sent a baby into this world . . .

People: . . . to redeem us. We could sing of God's unfailing love forever!

Leader: God sent the Messiah into this world . . .

People: to work for peace . . . to make possible reconciliation between creation and creature, between creature and creation. We could sing of God's unfailing love forever!

Leader: God sent Jesus, the Good Shepherd, the royal descendent of another shepherd king . . .

People: . . . from David, the humble shepherd boy turned heroic man with a heart that longed after God's own, who became the strong trunk of Jesus' family tree. We could sing of God's unfailing love forever!

Leader: And from these deep roots we all grow—grounded in love, working for peace in the name of Jesus, the Prince of Peace. Give praise to our Father in heaven. Cry out:

All: "You are my Father, my God, and the Rock of my salvation" (Psalm 89:26, NLT). We could sing of God's unfailing love forever!

Songs of Preparation: Planning team/worship leader can choose any combination of two or three songs to prepare the congregation to celebrate the peace that comes from being part of Jesus' family. Possibilities include "O God, Our Help in Ages Past," "Blessed Assurance," "I Go to the Rock," "Savior, Like a Shepherd Lead Us," "I Could Sing of Your Love Forever" (Smith and Martin), "Let the Peace of God Reign" (Zschech), "Shout to the Lord" (Zschech).

Individual Meditation

The worship leader should invite the congregation to enter into a time of individual meditation. They may remain seated or they may move to the two meditation stations set up in the worship space. The musicians need to provide approximately 15 minutes of meditative music for this portion. Before the last song, the worship leader should let the congregation know that this portion of the service is ending and they should return to their seats.

Congregational Guided Meditation

Leader reads from the Psalm 23 meditation from *The Complete Leader's Guide to Christian Retreats* by Rachel Gilmore or other peace-inspiring text of your choosing. Follow the directions for leading a guided meditation that are included in the meditation mentioned above(found online at www.judsonpress.com).

After reading the meditation, the reader should close with these words:

And Jesus said to his disciples, "My peace I leave with you; my peace I give to you. I do not give as the world gives. Do not let your hearts be troubled, and do not let them be afraid" (John 14:27, NRSV). Be of good courage and take those words to heart. God did not send his Son to create meaningless busywork in our lives, to complicate our already complicated human condition. God sent his Son to be at work in our lives that we might be at work in this world, passing on the peace he gives us, if we accept it and let it rule our hearts. Take the peace that Jesus gives you and go out into the world transformed.

Closing Song: "All Is Well" or "It Is Well with My Soul"

Note: Musicians should play meditative music for approximately 5–10 minutes following the service to allow people to be in prayer for peace. The planning team may also want to recruit prayer teams to be available for worshippers at the end of the service.

PART 2

Celebrations for All Generations

Want to fully engage all ages in learning about Advent together? Consider one of these intergenerational faith and fellowship programs designed to explore the history and traditions of Advent. Participants will form intergenerational small groups and work their way through two or three faith education stations where music, drama, stories, living histories, and other creative activities will reconnect them to the scriptural Christmas story in ways that get them (and keep them) thinking about this story's impact on our lives year round. Churches can easily adapt the programs to fit their needs by omitting stations as needed or simplifying the fellowship or worship components.

CHAPTER 8

Full Circle: An Advent Wreath Workshop

Key Verse: "For God loved the world so much that he sent his one and only Son, so that whoever believes in him will not perish but have eternal life" (John 3:16, NLT).

Purpose:
a. To introduce the biblical significance of Advent for Christians
b. To equip the congregation with daily devotional material to use at home
c. To provide outreach Advent devotional materials to Christmastime visitors and participants' friends, neighbors, and coworkers

Need-to-Know for Leaders

1. Planning for this event should start 3–4 months in advance, as there are supply costs to consider. Depending on how your church operates, you may need to charge participants a set fee or request a donation to offset wreath costs (about $7.00 to $10.00 per wreath, depending on whether candles are included).

2. The goal of this workshop is to make an Advent wreath for home, as well as one to give away, so each family unit is making two wreaths, not one, doubling the supply costs. Be sure to plan your budget accordingly.

3. Customize your materials list so that it fits your budget. Note that many craft stores offer weekly discount coupons that can be used to purchase and stockpile supplies, and the Internet has a wealth of discount craft supply sources.

4. Choose a date in mid- to late November or on the first Sunday of Advent so that wreaths and devotionals can be used on the first day of Advent.

5. Promote the event early and often. Be sure to include information about cost per household or suggested donations, as well as any requests for advance registration and/or for cookies or dessert for the fellowship portion.

6. For a shorter program, omit the Advent mixer or serve the refreshments during the gathering time before worship and making the wreaths. People can leave when they are finished with their wreaths.

Sample Schedule

2:50–3:20	Registration/Group Gathering
3:20–3:30	Worship
3:35–4:30	Advent wreath and devotional booklet activity
4:30–?	Fellowship with refreshments or optional full dinner

Gathering Time

What You'll Need

Volunteers: greeter/registrar, setup and cleanup crew

Christmas music and player

TV and DVD player with children's animated Christmas DVDs (optional)

Box of candy canes for Advent Mixer prizes

Photocopies of the Advent Mixer, one per person (see appendix)

Pens or pencils

Directions

1. Set up a registration table by the main door. Have a greeter/registrar seated 15 minutes before the event is scheduled to begin to check in participants and/or receive money. Also give an Advent Mixer handout to each participant (see reproducible handout in appendix). Younger children can team up with older youths or adults. Give people about 25 minutes to work on this activity, and award candy canes for the first three people or teams completing the sheet.

2. The planning team may choose to set up a TV and DVD player with children's animated Christmas programs showing in one corner of the gathering area and/or play Christmas music during the mixer time.

Worship

Note: Participants will move from the Group Gathering into this time of worship before making the Advent wreaths. This service is short and informal and can be done right in your gathering area.

What You'll Need

Volunteers: greeter/registrar, worship leader/ musician(s)

Photocopies or PowerPoint of carol lyrics

Advent wreath, candles, and matches or lighter

Photocopies or PowerPoint of order of worship

Order of Worship

Call to Worship

Leader: From the beginning of time, God was with us. God is with us.

People: Lord, let your light shine on us that we might be saved.

Leader: From Abraham, from Isaac, from Jacob, from Jesse, from David, from Isaiah, from Zechariah, God was with us. God is with us.

People: Lord, let your light shine on us that we might be saved.

Leader: From the lowly stable to the high hillsides, from the lakeshores to the dusty roads of Israel, God was with us. God is with us.

People: Lord, let your light shine on us that we might be saved.

Leader: From the cross to the tomb to the empty grave, God was with us. God is with us.

People: Lord, let your light shine on us that we might be saved.

Leader: From the hearts of the faithful through the ages, through the sufferings of the faithful through the ages, in times of trouble, in times of joy, God was with us. God is with us.

People: Lord, let your light shine on us that we might be saved.

Leader: From the first coming to the second coming of God's Son, God so loved this world that he sent his only Son to be with us—then, now, always.

All: Lord, let your light shine on us that we might be saved. Be here in this place with us now so that we might worship you. Come, Lord Jesus, come.

Opening Song: Choose one: "O Come, All Ye Faithful," "All Who Are Thirsty" (Brown).

Sharing the Advent Wreath

Leader reads or explains about the Advent wreath as preparation for the activity that follows.

Light has always been an important symbol for believers, especially in terms of the Christmas story. The Bible tells us that God created the world and brought light into the darkness, that Jesus is the Light of the World, that the angels surrounded the shepherds with a glorious, radiant light to announce the birth of Jesus, that the magi (often referred to as the wise men) followed the light of the star of Bethlehem to find Jesus and worship him. As Christianity developed, early Christians began to combine light symbolism with circles and greenery, symbolizing the eternal life-giving character of Christ, and the result was an Advent wreath. Christians have used Advent wreaths both at church and at home to help them mark the passage of time during Advent and focus their holiday preparations on Jesus' coming into this world two thousand years ago and Jesus' promised coming again. Using the wreath is simple. The wreath's four candles are lit, one week (or day) at a time and incorporated with Bible verses, prayers, songs, or meditations that can be shared around a dinner table or in a congregational worship setting. In a few minutes, we'll be making our own Advent wreaths and devotional books to use at home. We'll also be making a wreath and a shorter devotional book to give away to a friend, a neighbor, a family member, or a coworker. If you already have and use an Advent wreath, consider donating your "home" project tonight for the church to give away to visitors during the Advent season. Because God so loved the world, he gave us the gift of his Son, and spreading Christmas cheer really calls believers to share that good news with others.

Let's pray: *Lord, be with us now as we use our hands and hearts to make a gift that will help us worship you daily during Advent. We also ask that our wreaths that will be shared would give the gift of hope to someone who might not know you yet or wants to know you better. Use us so that we might share the love that you sent down at Christmas. These things we ask in the name of your precious Son, Jesus. Amen.*

Closing Song: Choose one: "Sing to the King" (Foote), "Away in a Manger," "What Child Is This?"

Faith Stations

Station 1. Advent Wreath and Devotional Booklets

What You'll Need

Volunteer: station host

12" straw wreaths (2 per household)

Set of 4 1" wooden candle cups with hole width that matches candle width if providing candles (2 sets of 4 per household)

Set of 4 10" taper candles—3 blue or purple, 1 pink— with a width that matches candle cups (2 sets of 4 per household)

1 package of inexpensive modeling clay (to help hold candles in cups if needed)

Wreath decorating supplies (colored wire star garland, artificial evergreen garland, eucalyptus branches, pine cones, artificial berry sprays, ribbon, etc.)

Low-temp hot glue guns and glue sticks

Scissors

Hole punches

Yarn or ribbon for binding booklets

Advent home devotional booklet (see reproducible download at www.judsonpress.com; 1 per household, plus 10–12 extra sets for families who already have a wreath at home but would like devotional materials)

Advent outreach devotional booklet (see reproducible pages in appendix or online at www.judsonpress.com; 1 per household for giveaway, ideally with a wreath)

Crayons and colored pencils (not markers)

Old newspaper for table coverings

Directions

1. In a large area (e.g., fellowship hall/gym), set up long worktables with six to eight chairs per table. Cover tables with old newspapers. Lay out wreath supplies (see above). Ideally, locate each worktable near an outlet for easy access to glue gun. Set each glue gun in a container to prevent accidental burns. Lay out the devotional book pages in order on another table with the hole punches and ribbon so that participants can easily collate their books.

2. After worship, invite people to move to the worktables. Watch for singles, young adults, or older adults who did not come with family groups. Be purposeful about mixing these participants with families at the tables. Once everyone is seated, ask one person at the table to plug in their glue gun.

3. Then ask participants to go around the table and share their name and the best Christmas gift they ever received. Allow 5–7 minutes for sharing before the station host explains the wreath/devotional book activity. Each household (whether family or single) will be making two wreaths and assembling two devotional booklets: a longer one to keep for home use and a shorter outreach version to give away. Participants who already have and use an Advent wreath may opt to give away both. Encourage families with multiple children to "lend" their children to those at their table who could use extra hands.

4. Wreath Instructions

a. Choose a straw wreath and decide how to decorate it. The wreath can be wrapped with artificial pine garland, tinsel star garland, or ribbon. Pine cones and eucalyptus branches can be hot glued on. Take a few minutes to plan, and then create!

b. Find four spots for the four candle cups and hot glue them in place.

c. Put a pebble-size lump of modeling clay in the bottom of each cup to help hold candles in place.

d. Repeat with the second wreath.

5. Booklet Instructions

a. Send volunteer(s) to the booklet table to assemble the devotional booklet pages in order, first for the home-use version, and then for the giveaway outreach version.

b. Punch three holes down the side of each assembled book.

c. Run a piece of ribbon/yarn through each hole and tie.

d. Sign the cover page of the outreach booklet as directed. Color the cover as desired.

Fellowship

What You'll Need

Volunteers: kitchen crew

Refreshments or dinner supplies per the planning team

Paper goods (cups, napkins, plates, etc.) and plastic-ware as needed for refreshments/meal

Directions

1. As people finish their wreaths and booklets, the station host can invite people to move into the fellowship area.

2. If you are holding the program on the first Sunday in Advent, consider opening your fellowship time with the first reading in the home version of the devotional booklet.

CHAPTER 9

Jesus' Family Tree

Key Verse: "A shoot will come up from the stump of Jesse; from his roots a Branch will bear fruit" (Isaiah 11:1, NIV).

Purpose:
a. To identify key people in Jesus' family tree
b. To connect our family histories to God's family tree
c. To take a next step in growing God's family tree

Need-to-Know for Leaders

1. This intergenerational program uses the idea of the Jesse Tree, which traces the family history of Jesus through story and art and has been part of the Christian tradition for more than a thousand years.

2. Relying on those same traditions, participants will move through three stations as a single group: Jesus' Family Tree, Family Fellowship, and Jesus' Family Tree Stories, which takes place in the context of worship.

3. While this program can be done at any point during Advent, hosting it earlier in the season will allow people to build on what they have learned and/or utilize the many online Jesse Tree resources provided for a month-long Advent devotional.

4. This program also includes fellowship time with food (snacks to pizza to a full dinner, depending on what the planning team decides). The planning team's decision will also determine whether or not the kitchen crew prepares part or all of the meal and if they need to charge participants a small fee to cover the costs.

5. The other unique feature of this program is that participants stay together, although divided into small groups for each station. If you do not have two large gathering areas, use multiple classrooms with duplicate sets of supplies in each for Station 1. Use your fellowship hall for the fellowship/eating station. Worship can be held in the fellowship hall or in your sanctuary if you have two separate spaces.

6. To shorten this program, omit the fellowship and refreshment component altogether.

Sample Schedule:

4:00–4:15	Gathering Time with Family History Facts
4:15–4:45	Jesus' Family Tree
4:50–5:20	Family Fellowship
5:25–6:00	Jesus' Family Tree Stories/Worship

Gathering Time

What You'll Need

Volunteers: greeter/registrar, station host, setup and cleanup crew

Photocopies of Family History Facts (see appendix for reproducible handout)

Pens or pencils

Directions

1. As people arrive and check in, give each household a Family History Facts handout and direct them to begin interviewing other participants to get their answers.

2. At the end of the gathering time, divide participants into small groups (ideally with 4–8 participants in each group) and send them to the Jesus' Family Tree station. (Use multiple classrooms with duplicate sets of supplies if needed.)

3. The kitchen crew should make sure that the eating area is set up for fellowship, as all participants will move from Station 1 to dinner and then to story time/worship as one group.

Faith Stations

Station 1. Jesus' Family Tree

What You'll Need

Volunteers: station host, station assistants (optional), musicians (optional)

Christmas music / player

12 6" paper leaves (cut from sturdy construction or scrapbooking paper)

Art supplies (crayons, markers, colored pencils, assorted trim, glitter, religious stickers, etc.)

Scissors

Glue sticks

Photocopies of the Jesse Tree Stories and Symbol Suggestions list (see handout in appendix)

Bibles

6'-8' piece of mural paper

Optional: instant camera/film or digital camera with printer cables and color printer

Optional: 3 6" bird shapes (cut from sturdy construction or scrapbooking paper)

Directions

1. The station host should welcome participants and invite them to gather at the worktables in their assigned groups then introduce the Jesse Tree:

The Jesse Tree is a symbol that comes out of the book of Isaiah in the Old Testament and has been represented in Christian art for more than a thousand years. The Jesse Tree is a reference to Jesse, the father of King David, who marks the official royal beginning of Jesus' earthly family history.

In Isaiah we read:

A shoot will come up from the stump of Jesse;
    from his roots a Branch will bear fruit.
The Spirit of the LORD will rest on him—
    the Spirit of wisdom and of understanding,
    the Spirit of counsel and of might,
    the Spirit of knowledge and fear of the LORD—
and he will delight in the fear of the LORD.

He will not judge by what he sees with his eyes,
    or decide by what he hears with his ears;
but with righteousness he will judge the needy,
    with justice he will give decisions for the poor
      of the earth.
He will strike the earth with the rod of his mouth;
    with the breath of his lips he will slay the wicked.
Righteousness will be his belt
    and faithfulness the sash around his waist.
      —Isaiah 11:1-5, NIV

Isaiah was telling the people about the Messiah, an anointed servant of God who would be born more than seven hundred years later and would deliver God's people. He would be a direct descendant, a great-great-great-great-great-great- (you get the idea) grandson of Jesse and Jesse's son King David. Christians have long identified this prophecy with Jesus, who was born centuries after Isaiah lived. Christian artists, over the centuries, created the Jesse

Tree as a way to remember the important people and stories that were part of Jesus' family tree, just as we're going to do now.

At your worktable, you have a handout with the list of important mothers and fathers in Jesus' family tree and selected Bible verses that tell their stories. Your group will be assigned one or more of the people. Your job is to read through the Bible passage in your group for each assigned person and then think of a symbol that could represent this person or story. You will then either use the art supplies to create that symbol on the leaf (or go on a hunt to find an object in the church, take a digital picture of it, and print it on the printer).

Make sure also to write the name of the person on the leaf and the Bible passage (book, chapter, verse). After our family dinner, we will be sharing these family stories in worship, so choose a volunteer(s) who will briefly explain the people on your leaves.

2. The host assigns Jesse Tree people to the various groups, and then the host and assistants help as needed. Groups have 30 minutes to work on creating their leaves before moving to dinner.

3. The host can play Christmas music as people work. Or if possible, invite musicians to play Christmas music. Participants may even sing along.

4. Participants who finish early can draw a large tree on the mural paper. (Fill the paper with a large tree trunk and leafy branches. Jesse Tree symbol leaves [and birds] will be placed on the tree during worship.)

Station 2. Family Fellowship

What You'll Need

Volunteers: station host, kitchen crew
Fellowship food for participants as chosen by the planning team
Paper goods
Participants' copies of the Family History Facts

Directions

1. The host should welcome participants and invite them to gather in their Station 1 groups at the tables. The host can combine groups or reassign as needed. Participants should have their copies of the Family History Facts with them, as the facts will provide structured dinner conversation.

2. The host should lead grace and then say: *As you eat tonight, ask your dinner companions the questions on the Family History Facts handout. You don't have to write down the answers; just enjoy the stories and know that together, all of us, brothers and sisters of Christ, make up the family of God.*

3. The host and kitchen crew eat with groups as able. After 30 minutes or so, the host should ask participants to clear their tables and proceed to the worship area where they should sit in their groups.

4. The host should gather the Jesse Tree leaves (and birds) from Station 1 and bring them with the Jesse Tree mural and double-stick tape to the worship area.

Station 3. Jesus' Family Tree Stories/Worship

What You'll Need

Volunteers: station host, worship leader/musician
Photocopies or PowerPoint of order of worship
Photocopies or PowerPoint of song/carol lyrics
Jesse Tree mural
Double-stick tape
Jesse Tree leaves (and birds)

Directions

1. The worship leader can welcome people and open worship with the first song.

2. The host should have the Jesse Tree leaves (and birds) and call up the groups' spokespersons so that the leaves can be placed on the family tree.

Note: The host should direct spokespeople to start toward the bottom of the branches and work their way up when placing their leaves/birds.

Order of Worship

Opening Song: Choose one: "Once in Royal David's City," "Earth Today Rejoices," "This Kingdom" (Bullock).

Call to Worship

Leader: Creator God, you are the God of Adam and Eve, Abraham and Sarah, Isaac and Rebekah.

People: The God of us all!

Leader: Eternal God, you are the God of Jacob and Leah, Judah and Tamar, Salmon and Rahab.

People: The God of us all!

Leader: Loving God, you are the God of Boaz and Ruth, David and Bathsheba, Solomon and Naamah.

People: The God of us all!

Leader: Mighty God, you are the God of Mary and Joseph.

People: The God of us all!

Leader: Creator God, you are the God of us all. You sent your Son, Jesus, to us, and we cry out:

All: "Abba, Father." We are your children, O God, and as your children, we are brothers and sisters of Christ Jesus. Generation upon generation, we come as your family to worship you!

Responsive Song: "O Come, O Come, Emmanuel" (selected verses) or "You Are Holy/Prince of Peace" (Smith)

Story Time: The host invites members of each group to come forward and share their leaf/leaves by giving the names of the mother and father, telling a little about them, and describing the symbol they chose to represent the pair. When finished sharing, the person should use the double-stick tape to attach the leaf to the Jesse Tree, starting at the bottom of the branches. The host should encourage children to be the volunteers for this activity as much as possible.

Closing Carol: "Joy to the World"

CHAPTER 10

Experiencing Advent through Carols

Key Verse: "The shepherds went back to their flocks, glorifying and praising God for all they had heard and seen. It was just as the angel had told them" (Luke 2:20, NLT).

Purpose:
a. To introduce/reintroduce traditional Christmas carols to all ages
b. To use the stories behind the songs to tell the Christmas story
c. To praise God and thank him for the gift of Jesus through song

Need-to-Know for Leaders

1. This program is a hybrid faith and fellowship/extended worship event. Ideally, the worship service takes place outside at night to recreate St. Francis of Assisi's very first Christmas Eve carol service. However, weather conditions will definitely impact the ability of your worshippers to stay outside for any length of time in December, as well as the ability of your instrumentalists to keep their equipment in tune and their fingers flexible. Feel free to stay indoors!

2. The program begins indoors with fellowship and refreshments. After checking in, participants can enjoy refreshments and conversation, watch *The Little Drummer Boy*, and/or complete the Carol History Trivia handout (see reproducible handout in appendix). Participants then move into a worship time, which can take place indoors in the same large gathering space, in your sanctuary, or outside.

3. For further background information on the history of carols, visit www.youtube.com/user/clancyrm and click on a carol title for a short, informative video on its story.

4. For a shorter program, simply pick and choose the carols whose history you want to share with your congregation and omit the rest, along with their readings.

What You'll Need

Volunteers: greeter/registrar, St. Francis of Assisi/narrator, multiple volunteer readers, worship leader/musician, kitchen crew (optional)

Christmas music / player

TV and DVD player

DVD of *The Little Drummer Boy* (Classic Media, 2007)

Photocopies of the Carol History Trivia handouts (1 per household; see reproducible handout in appendix)

Pencils

Worship service scenery (see description in Tech Notes below)

Photocopies of song sheets or PowerPoint of carol lyrics

Photocopies of lines for volunteer readers

Offering cards

Long gray or brown robe with tie for St. Francis

Optional: refreshments

Optional: paper goods

Directions

1. Ahead of time, set up the TV and DVD player in the gathering area for *The Little Drummer Boy* DVD and/or CD or MP3 player for Christmas music.

2. As people check in and gather, give each household a copy of the Carol History Trivia activity and encourage them to join forces with another group to complete the sheet before moving into worship.

3. Kitchen crew can provide refreshments during this time if using this option.

4. Members of the planning team should also use the gathering time to recruit volunteers to be readers in the worship service that follows.

5. The worship service is designed to recreate St. Francis of Assisi's very first Christmas Eve carol service in 1223 in Grecio, Italy. St. Francis, who was an unknown monk at the time, felt that people had lost touch with the Christmas story, so in the center of the village where there was a small rock outcropping, he set up a manger and brought an ox and a donkey and invited the people to come to church. He also adapted the pagan carols into laudas, Christmas songs that used familiar folk tunes and catchy rhythms to engage worshippers. These were the first Christmas carols to be sung at a Christmas Eve service almost eight hundred years ago.

6. Ideally, you will hold this service outside if weather allows. If the planning team can find a cow and a donkey to have present, even better. If not, ask children to play the animal roles.

7. Create a semicircular rocky cave out of gray garbage bags stuffed with newspaper, stacked up and connected with loops of duct tape, or paint a refrigerator box to resemble a rocky cave.

8. In the opening of the cave, place a wooden manger filled with straw. You can use this same setup indoors as well.

9. The service will introduce each carol listed on the history trivia sheet. St. Francis will serve as the overall leader for the service. Volunteer readers will present each carol, and then the congregation will sing a verse or two. Adapt as needed for length.

10. During the offering, the worship leader/musician can play a full version of one of the carols or other special music of his choosing. In lieu of a monetary offering, worshippers may be asked to give the pledge of their time (writing their names and contact information on an offering card) to go out Christmas caroling the following weekend or be part of a traveling worship service in the community (see chapter 15, "Advent"ure 1, page 70). Alternatively, they might bring the gift of a nonperishable food item or new/like-new winter clothing or blankets for distribution at a local food bank or shelter.

11. Assign greeters the task of handing out the offering cards to people as they enter worship. Be sure to also have pencils available for people to complete the cards.

Order of Worship

Welcome

St. Francis: *Benvenuto! Buon Natale!* Welcome! Merry Christmas! Tonight we gather to celebrate the birth of our King, Jesus. I am St. Francis of Assisi, a Franciscan monk who lived in Italy in the 1200s. While I was serving the church in Grecio, I began to feel as if people had forgotten the Christmas story. I wanted to make it come alive for them so they could experience the awe and wonder and majesty of the Christ Child's birth. I also knew that the little monastery chapel wouldn't be big enough to hold all the townspeople for the midnight Mass I was planning for Christmas Eve. So I wrote to the pope for permission to hold the service outside in the town square. There was a little gathering of rocks there that reminded me of the caves in Bethlehem. I got a manger with some straw and found a farmer to lend me an ox and a donkey, and I set up a worship space in this little rocky area in the center of town. When the people arrived, I began to read from the Gospel of Luke and preached to them about the good news the angels delivered that night. I also introduced Christmas carols into this midnight service. Carols were easy to sing and told the story of Jesus' birth in words the villagers could understand. It was a marvelous night. I was so overcome with emotion that I couldn't even say Jesus' name out loud; instead, I called him the Babe of Bethlehem. Will you join me now in singing a verse from "O Come, O Come, Emmanuel," one of the oldest Christmas carols still in existence, dating back to the church of AD 800?

Carol: "O Come, O Come, Emmanuel," verses 1 and 3 with refrain

Reader 1: "O Come, All Ye Faithful" has been sung with its present words and music for about three hundred years, although it spent its first hundred years with Latin words and the title "Adeste Fideles" and has several variations and additions to the verses. Let's sing verse 1 now.

Carol: "O Come, All Ye Faithful," verse 1 and refrain

Reader 2: "The Huron Carol," or "'Twas in the Moon of Wintertime," was actually written in the mid-1600s by St. Jean de Brebeuf, a Jesuit missionary to the Huron Indians in Canada. He used the Indians' native language and imagery to tell the story of Jesus' birth and share the amazing power of God's love with them. Let's sing a verse now. Even if you've never heard it before, listen to the words and think about how the word pictures might seem strange to you but would have appealed to the people with whom Father Jean was sharing God's Word. Let's sing it now.

Carol: "The Huron Carol/'Twas in the Moon of Wintertime," all 3 verses

Reader 3: "Joy to the World" was written by Isaac Watts, one of the most well-known hymn writers of the 1700s in England. He didn't write this hymn to be a Christmas carol. He wrote it as his interpretation of Psalm 98:4-9. A hundred years later, in 1839, American Lowell Mason published the words with a tune he had written, and "Joy to the World" began to make its way in the world as a Christmas carol. Let's sing a verse now.

Carol: "Joy to the World," verse 2

Reader 4: "Hark! the Herald Angels Sing" was written as a poem describing the events in Luke 2 in 1739 by Charles Wesley, brother of John Wesley, who founded the Methodist Church in England. The music didn't get attached to this famous carol until 1855,

when an organist named William Cummings took pieces of a Mendelssohn cantata and adapted them to fit the poem. Mendelssohn, a Jew, had said he didn't think that particular piece of music would ever fit a religious song. How wrong he was!

Carol: "Hark! the Herald Angels Sing," verse 1

Reader 5: "O Holy Night" was set to music by a Jewish composer named Adolphe-Charles Adam, who didn't believe that Jesus was the Son of God. The words were written in 1847 by Placide Cappeau, a French wine seller and poet, who later got angry with the church and turned away from his faith. How interesting that "O Holy Night" has become one of the most popular recorded and performed faith-based Christmas songs. In 1855 an American Unitarian minister named John S. Dwight translated "O Holy Night" into English. Also an antislavery activist, Dwight was particularly moved by the lyrics of verse 3. Let's sing that verse now.

Carol: "O Holy Night," verse 3 and chorus

Reader 6: "Go Tell It on the Mountain" also shares a theme of freedom and started out life as a slave song or African American spiritual. A choir director by the name of John Wesley Work spent the years following the Civil War collecting and preserving the spirituals and sharing them with his congregation so they could better understand their ethnic history. Work's son and grandson continued his musical research, and the version we know and sing now was published in 1940 by John Work III. This carol also tells the Christmas story found in Luke chapter 2.

Carol: "Go Tell It on the Mountain," verse 2 and chorus

Reader 7: "It Came upon the Midnight Clear" is probably the first well-known Christmas carol to be written in the United States. A Unitarian minister in Massachusetts, Rev. Edmund Hamilton Sears first published the lyrics as a Christmas poem in 1849. Music was added within a year or two, and "It Came upon the Midnight Clear" quickly became a popular addition to church Christmas services, strengthening the revival of Christmas celebrations in church and at home, which previously had been banned by the Puritans, both in England and here in the colonies.

Carol: "It Came upon the Midnight Clear," verse 3

Reader 8: A very grinchy thing happened to Katherine K. Davis, composer of "Carol of the Drum." Davis, an accomplished music teacher and pianist, wrote the carol in 1941. In December 1959, a friend called to tell her that radio stations all over the United States were playing her carol. Katherine had no knowledge of this, so she called the local radio station to ask what was going on. The station manager called back and told her that the carol was called "The Little Drummer Boy," and her name was not listed as an author. Eventually things got sorted out, and Katherine Davis's name was added to the list of composers for this very famous carol, which was also turned into an animated TV special in 1968.

Carol: "Little Drummer Boy," verse 1 and chorus

Reader 9: In April 1865, after President Abraham Lincoln had been assassinated, his body made a cross-country railroad journey as it traveled to its final burial place in Illinois. One of the stops along the way was Philadelphia, where half a million mourners came to pay their respects as President Lincoln's body lay in state. One of the mourners was a very well-known pastor named Phillip J. Brooks. Rev. Brooks was overwhelmed by the horrors and suffering of the Civil War and the vicious assassination of Lincoln. Needing spiritual renewal, in December of that year he made a pilgrimage to Bethlehem. He describes in his journal looking out over the Bethlehem hill country during the Christmas Eve service at the Church of the Nativity and finally being comforted by a sense of heavenly peace. Three years later, back in Philadelphia, Brooks wrote a poem called "O Little Town of Bethlehem," drawing on his memories of that Christmas Eve spent in the town where Jesus was born. Rev. Brooks shared the poem with the Sunday school students at his church. They loved it so much that Brooks asked the church organist to write music for the words. Although the organist procrastinated for many months, he did finish the song, and the Sunday school choir of the Church of the Holy Trinity first performed "O Little Town of Bethlehem" on December 27, 1868.

Carol: "O Little Town of Bethlehem," verses 1, 3, 5

Reader 10: The most famous, most sung, most recorded, most performed Christmas carol of all time is none other than "Silent Night." Lots of stories and legends swirl around the "true" history of this famous carol. The basic facts remain, however, that Father Joseph Mohr wrote the words to "Silent Night" in 1816 when he was the pastor of St. Nikola Church in Oberndorf, Austria. In 1818 he asked his friend and church organist Franz Gruber to write a simple guitar accompaniment so he would have a carol for Christmas Eve. "Stille Nacht! Heilige Nacht!" was born, but it wasn't until Bishop John Freeman Young, an American pastor, translated verses 1, 6, and 2 (in that order) and included them in an 1859 publication called *Carols for Christmas Tide,* that "Silent Night" began to find its way into the heart and soul of Christmas around the world.

St. Francis: *(Modify to fit your church's circumstances.)* As we come to the end of our service, we invite you to think about how you can "Go Tell It on the Mountain" this Advent. If you've enjoyed remembering and reliving the beauty and truth of these carols, we'd encourage you to join us for Christmas caroling next weekend. While we sing "Silent Night," the ushers will collect the offering. The only thing we're asking is the gift of your time. If you are willing to go out caroling or perhaps stay here at church and be part of the kitchen crew for the supper for the carolers, please write your name and contact information on the cards you received on the way in. All ages are welcome to join us, and you don't have to be choir-certified to attend! If you can't join us next weekend, consider hosting your own caroling party in your neighborhood (or nursing home or hospital or jail). Be like St. Francis and recreate Bethlehem in your community so that more people may experience the awe and wonder and majesty of the Christ Child's birth.

Carol: "Silent Night," three to six verses, depending on length of time needed for ushers to collect responses

St. Francis: People of God, remember that Christ was born in the City of David to bring you hope, to bring you love, to bring you joy, to bring you peace. Go tell it on the mountain and share the good news that Jesus Christ was born, not just for you, but for all people, to free us from our sin and live in friendship with God. *Andare con Dio. Buon Natale!* Go walk with God. Merry Christmas!

CHAPTER 11

Celebrating Small Things

Leader Need-to-Know

1. This intergenerational program uses two different stories to explore the idea of "small things" and how God rejoices over even the smallest things, especially small beginnings, because they indicate progress in our relationship with God. Instructions for an optional third story station are provided in case you have a large number of participants and need smaller rotation groups or you want to extend your program time.

2. During the station rotations, participants will be reflecting on a small thing they can give or a small beginning they can make in their friendship with God. These notes will be placed in small gift boxes, collected, and dedicated during the offering. The planning team will redistribute these to participants after Epiphany to remind the givers of their Christmas gift to Jesus and help hold them accountable.

Sample Schedule

4:00–4:15	Gathering Time
4:15–4:25	Welcome and directions
4:30–4:55	Station 1
5:00–5:25	Station 2
5:25–5:45	Regathering/fellowship time
5:45–6:00	Worship

*Note: Adding a third story station will extend your total time by 30 minutes.

Key Verse: "Do not despise these small beginnings, for the Lord rejoices to see the work begin" (Zechariah 4:10, NLT).

Purpose:
a. To focus on the "small things" in the Christmas story
b. To celebrate the "small things" God gives us in life
c. To offer a gift to God of "small things"

Gathering Time

What You'll Need

Volunteers: greeter/registrar, station host

Photocopies of holiday word searches/activity pages

Card or board games for children

Art supplies

Christmas music / player

Directions

1. Set up a few tables with art supplies and holiday activity pages and/or simple card and board games to occupy children during the opening registration time.

2. As soon as all people have signed in, the host can welcome the group and provide the following instructions:

Welcome! Today we're going to celebrate the gift of small things. God gave us the best small thing in the gift of the baby Jesus. From that tiny beginning of life, we received a gift that never stops giving, the gift of eternal life. Advent is a time to prepare to celebrate that amazingly small beginning, which seemed, on the surface, to be rather humble and insignificant. Yet listen to this verse from the prophet Zechariah, who ministered about five hundred years before Jesus' birth. He was giving encouragement to a faithful believer named Zerubbabel, who was going to rebuild the destroyed temple in Jerusalem. Even though Zerubbabel's efforts seemed small and he felt hopeless, Zechariah reminded him that God was pleased with his work: "Do not despise these small beginnings, for the LORD rejoices to see the work begin" (Zechariah 4:10, NLT). Keep Zechariah's encouragement in mind as you hear the two stories today. After each story, you will have a chance to think about a small gift you can offer Jesus this Christmas and will be invited to write this gift idea on a slip of paper. When you are finished with the stations, come back to the gathering area for the wrap-up activity and snacks. During closing worship, we will place our small gifts in the manger as an offering to baby Jesus. These gifts will be returned to you on Epiphany Sunday to remind you of the gift you gave Jesus and to encourage you to find more ways to keep giving yourself to Jesus. Let's prepare our hearts now to hear these stories of small gifts that please God with a carol about baby Jesus.

3. Sing first verse of "Away in a Manger"; a cappella is fine.

4. Have participants form two smaller groups and send one group to each station.

Faith Stations

Station 1. Come, They Told Him

What You'll Need

Volunteers: station host

TV and DVD player

DVD copy of *The Little Drummer Boy* (Classic Media, 2007)

Small slips of paper (1 per person)

Pens/pencils

Directions

1. The host welcomes participants, invites them to gather around the TV and DVD player, and introduces the DVD, saying: *The Little Drummer Boy is a story about a young orphan boy who ends up traveling with the three wise men to see baby Jesus. While the wise men are bringing the expensive and exotic gifts of gold, frankincense, and myrrh befitting an infant king, the little drummer boy thinks he has nothing of value to offer. But remember, God rejoices in even the smallest things.*

2. The host shows the DVD. When it's over, the host asks the group the following questions:

- Think about the gifts of the three wise men and then the gift of the drummer boy to the King. Why do you think God would rejoice over this small gift?
- What kind of a small beginning did it mark for the little drummer boy? Allow participants to answer.
- What kind of small gift of your talent could you offer to someone in Jesus' name this Christmas. (Examples: help an elderly neighbor address and send Christmas cards, put together a caroling group and visit a nursing home, arrange a Christmas bouquet and take it to someone whose day needs brightening, bake treats for the local police or fire department, help a single parent put up their Christmas tree or holiday lights, etc.)

3. The host then directs participants to write or draw that idea on one of the small slips of paper and take it with them to the next station.

Station 2. Another Stable Story

What You'll Need

Volunteers: station host

A copy of the book *Christmas Day in the Morning*
by Pearl S. Buck (HarperCollins, 2002, first
published in 1955)

Small slips of paper (1 per person)

Pens/pencils

Directions

1. The host welcomes participants and invites them to gather in a semicircle and introduces Pearl S. Buck's book *Christmas Day in the Morning*, saying: *Sometimes we feel that when we have no money to spend, we have no way to give a gift. In this story, a young farm boy thinks of a simple but dramatic way to give his father a gift to treasure. Remember, God rejoices in even the smallest things.*

2. The host then reads the story. When finished reading, the host asks the group the following questions:

- What did the young boy give to his father?
- Why do you think his father might remember that gift forever, above any other gift he might ever be given?

3. After allowing the group to answer the questions, the host asks: *What is a way you could offer the gift of time to someone in Jesus' name this Christmas by doing a job for someone, by doing a household chore without being asked, by simply spending time with a lonely neighbor, coworker, or family member?*

4. The host then directs participants to write or draw that idea on one of the small slips of paper and take it with them to the next station.

Optional: Station 3. To Be or Not to Be a Tree

What You'll Need

Volunteers: station host and station assistant

Copy of the book *The Tale of Three Trees* retold
by Angela Elwell Hunt (David C. Cook, 1989)
or *The Legend of the Three Trees* DVD (Thomas
Nelson, 2001)

Small slips of paper (1 per person)

Pens/pencils

Optional: TV and DVD player if using DVD

Directions

1. Ahead of time the host and assistant should read through *The Tale of Three Trees* several times and be familiar with each tree and its role. (Or simply use the DVD instead with the same introduction and follow-up questions.)

2. As participants arrive, the station assistant recruits volunteers from the group to be the three trees. (The assistant will coach volunteers as needed as they pantomime their roles to go along with the story text. Stand with arms in a circle or pointed down toward the floor for the young trees, fall to the ground when chopped down, become a boat/box/cross, etc.)

3. The host welcomes participants, invites them to gather in a semicircle, and introduces the story, saying: *Sometimes we dream of fancy, incredible gifts we can give to people we love, but fancy and incredible don't mean better. Remember, God celebrates small beginnings and small things.*

4. The host reads the story, allowing volunteers to act out parts with cues from the assistant, and then asks the group these questions:

- What if the trees had been used in the fancy, incredible ways they dreamed of when they were young trees standing in the forest?
- How were the "small things" they became much more important to Jesus?
- What small thing can you change in your life that will mark a new beginning in your friendship with Jesus? Examples: pray before dinner; memorize a new Bible verse each week; regularly clean my closet or pantry and make a donation to a local resale shop or homeless shelter; visit an elderly neighbor; share my toys willingly with my younger sibling, etc.

5. The host then directs participants to write or draw that change on a piece of paper and take it with them to the next station.

Station 4. Wrapping It Up

What You'll Need

Volunteers: station host, kitchen crew

Miniature boxes (jewelry-size, 1 per person)

Self-adhesive Christmas gift tags (1 per person)

Pens

Curling ribbon

Scissors

Refreshments

Paper goods

Optional: card or board games, art supplies,
    play dough for children

Directions

1. As participants return to the gathering area, the host should direct them to finish writing or drawing their gift ideas on the slips of paper they received at each station and then ask them to put the papers into a miniature box.

2. Have participants then fill out a self-stick gift tag: "To Jesus, From (insert first and last name)" and use it to seal the box. They should also tie a ribbon around the box to hold it closed.

3. Refreshments should be available during this time at the other end of the gathering area, and participants can enjoy fellowship until closing worship.

4. The planning team may also want to set out simple card/board games, drawing supplies, and/or play dough to occupy children until worship.

Worship

What You'll Need

Volunteers: worship leader/musician, additional reader
    (optional)

Photocopies or PowerPoint of order of worship

Photocopies or PowerPoint of carol lyrics

Manger big enough to collect participant gift boxes

Directions

Worship leader should invite participants to come to the worship area and bring their boxes with them.

Order of Worship

Opening Carol: "Away in a Manger," verses 2 and 3

Call to Worship

Leader: Be near us, Lord Jesus.

People: We ask you to stay.

Leader: Not only at Christmas.

People: But each and every day.

Reading: Matthew 25:31-40

Unison Prayer: Lord, we come to you, people caught up in the excitement of new, of big, of shiny, of fancy, of pricey, of more. Yet you sent us your Son, Jesus, as a baby to remind us that even though he was new to the world, he existed before Creation; that even though his birth was big news, his arrival was in a small stable surrounded by farm animals; that even though the magi brought shiny, fancy, pricey gifts fit for a king, Jesus only desires gifts from our hearts; that when we spend less time thinking about ourselves and more time sharing your Word, your Truth, and your love with others, that we give you the best gift of all—ourselves. As small as that may seem to us, help us to remember that you rejoice in and celebrate small things and new beginnings. Be at work in us, in our hearts and in our lives. Amen.

Offertory Carols: "In the Bleak Midwinter," verses 1, 2, and 5, and "Infant Holy, Infant Lowly" and/or "What Child Is This?" While congregation is singing, the worship leader invites people to come forward and place their gift boxes in the manger. The planning team should arrange to redistribute these to participants after Epiphany Sunday (first Sunday after the New Year).

Closing Prayer

Leader: Lord, please accept our gifts of small things that we have left here in the manger. You know what is in our hearts, Lord. You know what we are offering up to you or to our brothers and sisters in your name. Help us to honor you in all that we do and say, not just through these gifts, but in the way we live our lives. Amen.

Benediction

Leader: People of God, go out into the world and take that next step toward a new beginning in your friendship with Jesus. It is no small thing when you walk toward God and give to the world from the heart in Jesus' name. Know that in each small thing you do to honor him, God rejoices to see that work begin.

CHAPTER 12

The Peaceable Kingdom

Need-to-Know for Leaders

1. This intergenerational program explores animal theme Christmas legends from around the world and uses them to help participants understand Isaiah's image of the peaceable kingdom.

2. It features three stations with a time of worship and fellowship at the end of the program.

3. Remember to be intentional in creating the rotation groups, so that each group represents a cross section of your congregation in age and family makeup.

4. For a shorter program, serve refreshments during the gathering time and omit the fellowship component at the end. The planning team could also choose to use only 2 of the 3 stations.

Sample Schedule

4:00–4:15	Gathering Time
4:20–4:50	Station 1
4:55–5:25	Station 2
5:30–6:00	Station 3
6:05–6:20	Closing worship
6:20–7:00	Fellowship

Key Verse: "The wolf will live with the lamb, the leopard will lie down with the goat, the calf and the lion and the yearling together; and a little child will lead them" (Isaiah 11:6, NIV).

Purpose:
a. To understand how Christ will bring about the peaceable kingdom
b. To build unity of the Spirit in the bonds of peace within the church family and beyond
c. To explore animal legends related to the birth of Jesus

Gathering Time

What You'll Need

Volunteers: greeter/registrar, station host, setup and cleanup crews

Circle of chairs with one less chair than total number of players

Christmas music / player

Directions

1. As people check in, the host invites them to join in a game of Upset the Christmas Basket. (Rules follow below.) Keep adding chairs as needed for new players.

2. Chairs can also be used to set up two lines back-to-back for Musical Chairs.

3. The three Christmas Basket teams can be used as the station rotation groups too.

Upset the Christmas Basket Rules

1. Create a circle of chairs, one per player, and then take away one chair. As new people arrive, incorporate them by adding chairs after each round.

2. Find a volunteer to be in the middle (no chair).

3. Using three names of characters or items from the Christmas story (e.g., three magi/wise men, three shepherds, three angels), go around the circle and assign one identity or item to each person. For example, the first person would be *shepherd,* the second would be *magi,* and the third would be *angel,* and so on around the circle. Or assign the items gold, frankincense, and myrrh instead.

4. The person in the middle then calls out one of the groups, such as shepherds, and all people assigned to that group jump up and switch seats. Whoever doesn't find a seat must take the middle spot.

5. The middle person may also call out, "Upset the Christmas basket," which means that *all* players must jump up and switch seats. Whoever is without a seat takes the middle position, and a new round begins. (Be sure to take precautions if you have seniors, people with disabilities, or very young children playing this game.)

Faith Stations

Station 1. Animals of the Nativity

What You'll Need

Volunteer: station host

A large tabletop nativity set

PDF copies of "The Donkey's Bray," "The Robin," "The Stork," and "The Camels" from *Legends and Traditions of Christmas* by Trudie West Revoir and John Pipe (rev. ed., Judson Press, 1998), available online at www.judsonpress.com

Small replicas/models of a robin, a stork, a donkey, and one or more camels

Note: The robin can be purchased from a craft supply store. The stork can be purchased online [search "stork decoration"] or made out of poster board (body), orange pipe cleaners (legs and beak), and white craft feathers (decorate body). The donkey and camels can be taken from an existing nativity set.

Directions

1. The station host welcomes participants and invites them to gather around the nativity set, which can be set up on a small table in front of the host.

2. The host introduces the stories, saying the following:

In the Christmas story in the Bible, we read about shepherds keeping watch over their flocks and about Mary placing Jesus in a manger, which is an animal's feedbox. We assume that because Jesus was laid in a manger, stable animals, such as cows, sheep, goats, and donkeys, must have been nearby. Bible scholars also believe that the magi who followed the star to Jesus' birthplace likely traveled by camel caravan since it was a long journey across the desert. It is probable, too, that Mary and Joseph joined a caravan of fellow travelers heading to Bethlehem for the census and that Mary rode a donkey instead of walking the eighty miles. However, over the years, storytellers added creatively to the original biblical narrative, placing a robin and a stork in the stable, each with its own role in greeting the infant king. The camels are given amazing travel powers as a reward for their faithful trek through the desert, and the donkey develops his unique bray through his interaction with the holy family. While these legends are made up of stories passed down over time, their truth lies in the heart of their message—that all living creatures serve the Lord and worship him with gladness. Listen to these stories and see what truth you take away.

3. The host picks up the robin and places it on the roof of the stable or near the holy family and reads (or tells) "The Robin" excerpt.

4. The host follows this pattern with the stork, the camels, and the donkey.

5. Then the host asks, *What did each animal give that only it could give?* (Robin—wings fanned the flames to warm the baby. Stork—gave up her feathers to keep the baby warm. Camels—faithfully persevered even though they were tired, hungry, and thirsty, to carry the magi to the baby. Donkey—used its voice to warn of danger.) *If you were an animal present for Jesus' birth, what would you be and what gift would you give that only you could offer?* Allow participants time to discuss in small groups, and then call on people to answer.

6. The host may close the activity by leading the group in an a cappella verse of "Joy to the World" and giving thanks for the individual gifts and talents with which God has blessed each believer.

Station 2. The Lamb's Gift

What You'll Need

Volunteer: station host

Copy of *The Crippled Lamb* by Max Lucado (Thomas Nelson, 1994)

CD or MP3 player

CD or MP3 recording and photocopies of lyrics for the Shaker hymn "Simple Gifts"

Directions

1. The host welcomes participants and invites them to gather in a semicircle and introduces the book, saying: *Sometimes we feel like we have nothing to offer God—that we're not big enough, not strong enough, not smart enough, not rich enough to give God a worthy gift. In this story, Joshua the lamb learns that simply being who is he is exactly the gift Jesus wants from him.*

2. The host reads the story. When finished reading, the host asks the group the following questions:

- Why did Joshua think he had nothing to offer the baby?
- How did his being different allow him to give a different kind of gift?
- What makes you different from your friends/coworkers/family members?
- What kind of personal gift can you give that would warm someone's heart?

3. The host allows participants to discuss in small groups for 5–10 minutes and then asks for a few volunteers to share their answers with the large group.

4. The host closes the station by playing "Simple Gifts" and offering a simple prayer asking God to place us where we need to be so that we might share our blessings with the world.

Station 3. The Peaceable Kingdom

What You'll Need

Volunteer: station host

Bibles and/or photocopies of Isaiah 11:1-9 (one per household)

An 8'–12' sheet of mural paper with a tree stump drawn in the middle of it

Markers

A sheet of poster board labeled "Peace Prayer" with the words "I pray for peace . . ." written at the top

CD or MP3 player

CD or MP3 recording and/or photocopies of lyrics for "Let There Be Peace on Earth"

Directions

1. The host should welcome participants, invite them to gather in a semicircle, and introduce the Isaiah passage, saying: *The prophet Isaiah told the Israelites about God's plan to bring a savior to the world from the family of King David, whose father was Jesse. Eventually a young woman would give birth to a baby who would be King of the universe, who would seek righteousness, bring justice, and rule the world with peace. Listen to what he says. . . .*

2. The host reads Isaiah 11:1-9 and then asks the participants to break into small groups of six to eight people and answer these questions: *Where do you see*

the need for the peaceable kingdom right now? In your family? In your workplace? In your school? In your community? In the world?

3. The host allows groups 5–10 minutes to discuss and then asks: *Isaiah says, "And a little child shall lead them." Jesus said something similar in a very different context when he told his disciples, "Unless you become like a little child, you won't see the kingdom of heaven; it belongs to children like this." (See Matthew 18:3; 19:14.) What makes a child so significant in God's peaceable kingdom? Why do you think Scripture associates children with peace—in Isaiah and even in the Beatitudes? (See Matthew 5:9.) How can we follow that example and work for peace in this world?*

4. The host allows groups 5–10 minutes to discuss and then invites people to add to the "Stump of Jesse" mural where they can draw (or write the words for) two normally opposite/conflicting things (people, animals, countries, cultures, etc.).

Note: The host can refer participants back to the Isaiah 11:1-9 passage to give them ideas.

5. The host also invites people to add requests to the peace prayer, which will be used during worship (e.g., "I pray for peace . . . in my family, in the Sudan, with my mother, in my school, etc.").

6. The host closes the session by playing and/or leading the group in singing "Let There Be Peace on Earth."

Worship

What You'll Need

Volunteers: worship leader/musician, additional
   reader (optional)
Photocopies or PowerPoint of order of worship
Photocopies or PowerPoint of carol lyrics
Manger

Directions

The worship leader should invite participants to come to the worship area and distribute song sheets and order of worship if needed.

Order of Worship

Opening Song: "Doxology" (traditional or David Crowder Band)

Responsive Reading: Isaiah 11:1-9, NIV

Leader: A shoot will come up from the stump of Jesse; from his roots a Branch will bear fruit.

People: The Spirit of the LORD will rest on him—the Spirit of wisdom and of understanding, the Spirit of counsel and of might, the Spirit of knowledge and of the fear of the LORD—

Leader: And he will delight in the fear of the Lord. He will not judge by what he sees with his eyes, or decide by what he hears with his ears;

People: But with righteousness he will judge the needy, with justice he will give decisions for the poor of the earth. He will strike the earth with the rod of his mouth; with the breath of his lips he will slay the wicked.

Leader: Righteousness will be his belt and faithfulness the sash around his waist.

People: The wolf will live with the lamb, the leopard will lie down with the goat, the calf and the lion and the yearling together; and a little child will lead them.

Leader: The cow will feed with the bear, their young will lie down together, and the lion will eat straw like the ox.

People: The infant will play near the cobra's den, and the young child put its hand into the viper's nest.

All: They will neither harm nor destroy on all my holy mountain, for the earth will be full of the knowledge of the LORD as the waters cover the sea.

Unison Prayer: Creator God, at Christmastime we sing "Joy to the world . . . Let heaven and nature sing." And yet we forget that you are the one who brings us joy. We forget that even the rocks cry out at the sound of your holy name and that all of creation bows down to you. Lord, we want to give all glory and honor to you. Be gracious with us. Forgive us when we turn away from you, from our neighbor, from those who need to know who you are. We especially pray tonight, Lord, for your return and the fulfillment of the peaceable kingdom—of peace on earth, goodwill to all people. Hear our prayers for peace. *(Leader reads from poster board created in Station 3.)* These things we ask in the name of our Prince of Peace, Wonderful Counselor, Everlasting Father, Mighty God. Amen.

Closing Song: "Go Now in Peace" or "Dona Nobis Pacem" (sing as a round if possible)

Fellowship

What You'll Need

Volunteers: kitchen crew

Refreshments

Paper goods (consider purchasing cups/plates with an animal theme)

CD or MP3 player

CD or MP3 recording of Randall Thompson's "The Peaceable Kingdom"

Directions

1. After the closing song, the worship leader should invite participants to stay for a time of fellowship and refreshments.

2. The planning team may choose to play Thompson's "The Peaceable Kingdom" during fellowship.

CHAPTER 13

Good News for All People

Key Verse: "But the angel said to them, 'Do not be afraid. I bring you good news of great joy for all the people'" (Luke 2:10, NIV).

Purpose:
a. To explore other countries' Christian Christmas traditions
b. To understand that God intended the good news of Christmas to be shared with all people
c. To value cultural Christmas legends as fictional stories that offer spiritual truths when read from a Christian perspective

Need-to-Know for Leaders

1. This intergenerational program uses Christmas legends and traditions from Christians around the globe to celebrate the good news of Jesus Christ that God intends for all people. The planning team and facilitators should be very clear with participants that the legends that have traveled through generations of cultures are fictional stories; however, when viewed through the Christian lens, they offer valuable spiritual truths that can enhance our celebration of Christmas.

2. For the fellowship time, the planning team should recruit volunteers to bring Christmas treats from other cultures and countries. The team can supplement these refreshments as needed or just supply the punch, coffee, and paper goods.

3. If your church has connections to sister churches or neighborhoods with immigrant populations, invite one or more of these groups to participate with you from the planning stages through the final clean up. Share the Good News!

4. For a shorter program, omit the final fellowship and refreshments component or choose only 2 of the 3 stations.

Sample Schedule

4:00–4:20	Gathering Time
4:20–4:25	Welcome and directions
4:25–5:00	Station 1
5:05–5:35	Station 2
5:40–6:05	Station 3
6:10–6:30	Worship
6:30–7:00	Fellowship

Gathering Time

What You'll Need

Volunteers: greeter/registrar, station host, setup and cleanup crew

Christmas around the World display items (see items listed directly below)

Tables set up in gathering area for these displays

A lettered sign for each display (do not write the country name!)

Photocopies of the Christmas around the World handout (see reproducible handout in appendix)

Pencils

Directions

1. Ahead of time, the planning team should set up the Christmas around the World items in the gathering area, which will also serve as Station 3. Make a sign with a letter, not the country name, for each group of items, as teams will be trying to figure out the country of origin. Items are as follows:

A. sprig of fresh basil tied to a small wooden cross and set in a small bowl of water (Greece)

B. bunch of thorny branches interspersed with red, orange, and yellow streamers or cellophane strips to resemble small bonfire; candles; a Bible open to Psalm 98 (Iraq)

C. small tabletop Christmas tree decorated with Chinese paper lanterns (available at craft supply stores), paper flowers (can be made from colored tissue paper), and paper chains (China)

D. large gold paper star lanterns (or stars) strung on a rope; nativity set; poinsettia flowers; small clay oil lamp (India)

E. 3' dowel rod or stick with a foil-wrapped star glued to the top. Place a picture of the holy family in the center of the star. Glue lengths of ribbon hanging down from the star. Attach a few bells to the ribbons or glue to the star. (Romania)

F. roller skates, firecrackers, bells, 8'–10' length of string (Venezuela)

G. handbells to represent church bells, a January calendar page with January 7 circled, tabletop Christmas tree, holiday lights (Egypt)

H. candles, white sheet with colorful stripes fabric painted onto the ends, flatbread, a January calendar page with January 7 circled (Ethiopia)

2. As people arrive and check in, give each household a Christmas around the World handout and ask them to look at the lettered items in the gathering area and try to guess which country uses them in their Christmas celebrations.

3. Households can join forces and work together as a team or a planning team member can begin creating rotation groups and encourage people to work as a team on this first activity.

4. At the end of the gathering time, divide participants into three groups (if not already divided) and send them to the three faith stations.

Faith Stations

Faith Station 1. Babushka–Always Searching

What You'll Need

Volunteer: station host/storyteller (ideally a female)

PDF copy of the Babushka excerpt from *Legends and Traditions of Christmas* by Trudie West Revoir and John Pipe (rev. ed., Judson Press, 1998), available online at www.judsonpress.com, or for a slightly different retelling, visit www.mikelockett.com/stories.php?action=view&id=34

Shawl and scarf for storyteller's costume

3 small gifts (e.g., a snow globe, a piece of candy, a baby blanket)

Optional: a piece of candy for each child participant

Long winter scarf

Safety pins

Small pieces of paper (approximately 3" x 3")

Pens

Audio recording of "I Wonder as I Wander" and/or "We Three Kings of Orient Are"

Note: The Revoir and Pipe excerpt involves shepherds, while the online version retold by Lockett features the three magi, as do most other retellings. Because there are slight differences, the storyteller should be familiar with whichever version the planning team decides to use.

Directions

1. The host/storyteller should welcome participants and invite them to gather in a semicircle and introduce the legend, saying: *Babushka is a Russian word meaning both "grandmother" and "scarf." See my scarf? I am a grandmother who is going to tell you the legend of Babushka, a little Russian grandmother who was invited to go see the baby Jesus. But did she go? Let's find out.* Storyteller reads or tells the Babushka story, using the gift props at the end as appropriate. Alternatively, she should give a piece of candy to each child.

2. After the story, the storyteller asks the group to divide into groups of six to eight people and says: *Babushka made a choice in not going with the shepherds/magi to see the baby Jesus, which affected the rest of her life. Have you ever made a choice that later you wished you hadn't? How did that choice affect your life? Tell your group about it.*

3. The host allows groups to discuss and then asks: *If you were invited to travel with the shepherds/magi to see Jesus, would you have just picked up and left your house? If you had gone, what gift would you have brought the baby?*

4. The host allows groups to discuss and then asks: *The legend says that Babushka never stopped looking for the baby Jesus. She lived a life of sadness, thinking that Jesus could never be a part of her life. Sometimes we become like Babushka. We live in the past and forget that Jesus died to erase our sins, mistakes, and regrets. Take a minute to think about a sad choice you made in your life. When you think of it, write it on a slip of paper, fold it over, and pin it to the scarf. We're going to give all those regrets and sad choices to Jesus so we can celebrate Christmas with the joy that comes from seeking his forgiveness and living in his love for us.*

5. The host lets participants work and assists them in pinning the papers to the scarf as needed (being sensitive to the needs of children and of people who may have tremors or arthritis), and then closes the session by playing the recording of "I Wonder as I Wander" or "We Three Kings of Orient Are" and offering a blessing as the group moves on.

Station 2. Saint Lucia—A Light in This World for God

What You'll Need

Volunteer: Station host

PDF copy of the Saint Lucia excerpt from *Legends and Traditions of Christmas* by Trudie West Revoir and John Pipe (rev. ed., Judson Press, 1998), available online at www.judsonpress.com, or a Saint Lucia picture book, such as *Lucia, Saint of Light* by Katherine Bolger Hyde (Conciliar Press, 2009)

3–5 Saint Lucia wreaths (Use artificial evergreen garland to make 6" wreaths. Tape or hot glue 6–8 birthday candles around the wreath or make candles from colored pipe cleaners.)

Plates of coffee cake (need 3–5 total plates for servers with 1 small piece of cake per person)

Napkins

Directions

1. The host welcomes participants, invites them to gather in a semicircle, and introduces the legend, saying: *The legend of Santa Lucia or Saint Lucia is the story of a Christian girl in Italy who lived about three hundred years after Jesus was born. Her refusal to give up on her faith made her famous, and over the years, special traditions developed to help people remember and honor her faithfulness. Let's find out more.*

2. Read the excerpt or picture book. When finished reading, the host asks participants to break into smaller groups of six to eight people and says: *Who is one person whose faith you admire? Tell your group about that person.*

3. Allow participants to discuss this for 5–10 minutes, and then ask each group to send a volunteer (ideally the oldest female child or teen, but any age or gender may play the part) to the front. The host places a candle crown on each girl's head and says: *One of the Saint Lucia traditions in Sweden is that on December 13, Saint Lucia Day, the oldest daughter prepares coffee and coffee cake for the family, dresses up in a red or white robe and a candle crown, and then serves her family breakfast in bed. Real Saint Lucia girls wear crowns with lit candles. We're not going to light our crowns, but our Saint Lucias will serve their groups coffee cake.*

4. The host directs *Saint Lucias* to pass out napkins and then coffeecake to their groups. Then host says: *While you eat, think about Lucia and her gift of faithfulness. What is one way you can show your faithfulness to Jesus, not just at Christmastime but throughout the year? Share these ideas with your group.*

5. The host allows groups to eat and talk. After 5–10 minutes, the host can close with a reading or group singing of "Break Forth, O Beauteous Heavenly Light" or "This Little Light of Mine" and give an encouragement to go out and be lights in this world for Jesus.

Station 3. Christmas Celebrations around the World

What You'll Need

Station host

Copy of Christmas around the World handhout for host, plus answer key (see right)

Access to Christmas around the World display items

Guest speakers to represent other cultures (e.g., nations/tribes of Africa, Asia, Latin and South America, Eastern Europe, etc.)

Directions

1. Ahead of time the planning team should recruit one or two guest speakers from your local congregation or community who are first-generation immigrants or who are still in touch with the culture of their country of origin. You may also find such speakers through denominational resources or other personal contacts. Find Christians who are familiar with religious Christmas celebrations in other countries either from living or working there. Invite these speakers to talk to your group about how Christians celebrate Christmas in the part of the world they represent. They can bring "show and tell" objects to help them. These speakers can provide input in addition to the information presented in the quiz.

2. As participants arrive at the station, the host should welcome them and invite them to gather in a semicircle and take out their Christmas around the World handouts. The host will review the answers by holding up the lettered items and reading from the answer key at right. If a guest speaker represents one of the quiz countries, that person can present the information instead of the host.

3. After reviewing the quiz answers, the host should invite the guest speakers to come forward and share their Christmas experiences with the group. The host can facilitate group questions afterward.

Christmas around the World Answer Key

A. At Christmastime Christians in Greece tie a sprig of fresh basil to a small wooden cross and hang it in a bowl of water to keep the basil fresh. The mother in the house then dips the basil in holy water each day and sprinkles the water in each room to keep away evil spirits. The basil on the cross is the main symbol of the season, like our Christmas tree. Christmas gifts are also exchanged on St. Basil's day, January 1. (According to Greek history, St. Basil was a wealthy man who gave away all of his possessions to those in need. He is one of two forefathers of the modern day Santa Claus, the other being Nicholas, another Greek saint.) On Christmas Eve children travel from house to house singing *kalanda,* which are like Christmas carols. Families celebrate Christmas Day with a big feast, because in Greece people fast from eating meat for the forty days before Christmas. (Eastern Orthodox churches, including the Greek Orthodox Church, still honor Advent as a penitential season, much like the season of Lent. In the West and especially in the United States, Christians have gotten away from that tradition in the church year.) One of the special foods at the feast is *cristopsomo,* or "Christ bread," a yeast bread that comes in different sizes and shapes and is decorated with a symbol that represents the family's professions (carpenter, fisherman, cook, clothing merchant, etc.).

B. On Christmas Eve Christian children in Iraq read the Christmas story from the Bible while the adults hold candles. After the story, they light a small bonfire made from a pile of thorny twigs and read a psalm while the fire burns. On Christmas Day Christians go to church and celebrate with another bonfire while the men in the congregation chant a hymn. Afterward the bishop carries an icon of the Christ Child on a scarlet cushion and leads a processional outside the church. The service ends with the "touch of peace," which is passed from person to person until all people have received the blessing. In 2008 the Iraqi government declared Christmas an official holiday.

C. Christians in China represent only 1 percent of the population, so in the past, many Christians have celebrated privately. However, because Christianity is growing there, midnight worship services often overflow the local churches. These days it is also common for Chinese Christians to decorate their homes with a tree of lights that features paper lanterns, flowers, and chains.

D. In India, Christians represent less than 3 percent of the population, yet Christmas is a popular holiday in the country. Indian Christians faithfully attend church on Christmas Eve and like to decorate their homes with poinsettias and nativity sets. In some communities, residents string huge gold paper star lanterns on ropes between the houses so that entire streets are lit by stars. In other parts of India, Christians set out small clay oil lamps on the flat roofs of their homes to symbolize that Jesus is the Light of the World.

E. In Romania on Christmas Eve, Christians go from house to house following a leader who carries a *steaua*, which is a foil star featuring a picture of the holy family and decorated with bells and ribbons attached to the top of a big stick. Songs and stories are told and sung at each house along the way, and the visitors receive treats from the homeowners. This religious tradition was followed for hundreds of years until Romania surrendered to the former Soviet Union during World War II and became a Communist country. When Romania received its independence in 1989, Christian holiday traditions slowly began resurfacing and are growing in popularity again.

F. In Venezuela Christians observe a nine-day preparation period before Christmas. Part of this preparation involves getting up early to go to church every morning. In the capital of Caracas, Christians have an unusual tradition of roller skating to church every morning. Streets are closed to cars until 8:00 a.m. to allow the roller skaters safe passage. Young children go to bed early during this preparation time but tie a string around their big toes and hang the strings out their windows. The roller skaters tug on the strings to wake the children up early for church. Firecrackers and bells also signal that early church services are starting. During the season, Christian homes are typically decorated with lights, Christmas trees, and nativity sets called *nacimientos*.

G. In Egypt, the population is predominantly Muslim. Those who are Christian are mostly part of the Eastern Orthodox Church. These Coptic Christians celebrate Christmas on January 7. Advent for Coptic Christians is 43 days long, beginning November 25. During that time, most Christians fast from meat, dairy, and eggs, especially for the last week. On Christmas Eve, people go to church dressed in new clothes. The church bells are rung at the end of the service to signal the arrival of Christmas Day. People then return home and eat a special meal called a *fata*, made of boiled meat, garlic, and rice. For both Coptic Christians and Western Christians in Egypt, Christmas trees and holiday decorations are displayed.

H. In Ethiopia, Christians are part of the Eastern Orthodox Church and celebrate Christmas (called Ganna) on January 7. On the morning of Ganna, people get up and dress in a traditional white toga-type garment which has bright stripes on the ends. (Residents of bigger cities and towns may simply wear regular clothing.) At church, each worshipper is given a candle, and the service starts with chanting and singing. After church, people celebrate with a traditional meal made up of *wat*, a meat stew served on *injera*, a flatbread that is used to scoop up the stew.

Worship

What You'll Need

Volunteers: worship leader/musician, additional reader (optional)

Photocopies or PowerPoint of order of worship

Photocopies or PowerPoint of carol lyrics

Wooden cross (approximately 6' tall, homemade from two large branches or 2" x 4" lumber)

Directions

1. Worship leader should invite participants to come to the worship area.

2. The host from Station 1 should bring the scarf with all the participant choices pinned to it.

Note: If you have invited guests from other cultures, ask them to share the lyrics of the carols in their native language and/or sing the verses in their native language. Your guests may also be able to suggest additional foreign language carols to include.

Order of Worship

Opening Carol: "Hark! the Herald Angels Sing" verses 1–3

Call to Worship

Leader: People of God, at Jesus' birth the angels proclaimed the Good News.

People: This is good news for all people!

Leader: Jesus Christ was born in Bethlehem for me, for you, for all of God's children everywhere.

People: This is good news for all people!

Leader: Jesus Christ entered our world as a baby but became our victorious King, working on our behalf to save us from our sin and from the sins of the world.

People: This is good news for all people!

Leader: At Christmastime we sing songs that tell the angel's message: "Do not be afraid. I bring you good news that will cause great joy for all the people. Today in the town of David a Savior has been born to you; he is the Messiah, the Lord" (Luke 2:10-11, NIV). This is the good news that will bring great joy to all people. May all who have ears to hear, hear the good news!

All: We have heard the good news. Joy to the world! The Lord is come! Amen.

Reading: Luke 2:8-20

Responsive Carol: "Go Tell It on the Mountain"

Reading: Matthew 28:18-20

Unison Prayer: *(Station 2 host wraps the scarf around the cross as the people pray.)* Lord, we come to you, people of hope and people of fear; people of joy and people of sadness; people of love and people of hate; people of peace and people of conflict. We give to you now those pieces of our lives, those choices we've made that we regret, that have brought us sadness, that have brought you sadness when we've turned away from your words, your wisdom, and your will for our lives. Take these chains that bind us, Lord, that prevent us from going and sharing the good news of your truth and your love. Break these chains that hold us back, Lord, and set us free to live a life worthy of the one to which you've called us, a life in which we walk in this world proclaiming the good news of your birth and bringing joy to others as we discover your love for us all. May all who have ears hear.

Closing Carol: "Glory to God" or "Rise Up, Shepherd, and Follow"

Fellowship

What You'll Need

Volunteers: kitchen crew

Refreshments (hot and cold beverages; assorted desserts and snacks, ideally representing foods from various cultures)

Paper goods

Christmas music / player

Directions

1. After worship invite participants back to the gathering area for refreshments.

2. The team should facilitate visiting between congregation members and any invited guests.

3. The team may choose to play Christmas carols recorded in multiple languages as background music.

PART 3

Special Celebrations

Is your congregation ready for an "Advent"ure this Christmas season? Then consider one of these special celebrations. From exploring Advent through the arts to taking Advent to the streets of your community to an Advent game show based on "The Twelve Days of Christmas" song, your congregation will experience the Christmas story like never before. The goal of these entertaining, yet educational celebrations is to unite your church family and help them understand the Christmas story as part of the never-ending story that has shaped God's people from generation to generation, from Adam and Eve to you and me and to our children's children. Churches can easily adapt programs by omitting stations or simplifying fellowship options, as needed.

CHAPTER 14

An Advent Arts Celebration

Find "More Advent Arts to Celebrate" online at www.judsonpress.com!

Key Verse: "My soul magnifies the Lord, and my spirit rejoices in God my Savior" (Luke 1:46, NRSV).

Purpose:

a. To explore Advent themes through Christmas music (secular, religious traditional, religious contemporary)

b. To explore Advent themes through visual art

c. To explore Advent themes through storytelling/drama

d. To create worship resources to be used throughout Advent in Sunday worship (banners, songs, prayers, dramas, etc.)

Need-to-Know for Leaders

1. Schedule this intergenerational event early in Advent (or even just prior) so that the resources created can be used in worship services during the remainder of the season. Be sure to emphasize that all congregation members and guests of all ages are invited, whether they have children living at home or not. Help create community by pairing up older adults with young families or several single adults with couples or smaller families.

2. While this program has three stations (for a shorter, simpler event, choose just one or two stations), the format is free flow, in that participants can visit any and all stations and work on the projects that interest them most. The planning team should circulate throughout the event and remind people that they can try additional stations/activities.

Note: If your church has already selected a Christmas play that requires scenery, the planning team can coordinate with the play directors to rehearse and/or create scenery during this workshop time. Just add in the appropriate supplies and volunteers to the Visual Arts and Drama stations.

Sample Schedule

2:50–3:15	Registration/Gathering time/Fellowship
3:15–3:30	Worship
3:30–5:00	Station Rotations

Gathering Time

What You'll Need

Volunteers: kitchen crew, setup and cleanup crew
Refreshments
Paper goods
Christmas music / player

Directions

1. As participants arrive and check in, have Christmas music playing and refreshments available.

2. When you are ready to begin, a station host from each area should give an overview of the activities available at his or her station.

3. The worship leader can begin worship as soon as the general directions for the evening are given.

Worship

What You'll Need

Volunteers: worship leader/musician
Photocopies or PowerPoint of carol lyrics
Photocopies or PowerPoint of order of worship

Order of Worship

Opening Carol: "Glory to God"

Reading: Exodus 35:4-45

Unison Prayer: Lord, you created us as unique individuals, each with our own talents and abilities. So often we forget that our blessings can be used to build up your kingdom and give glory and honor to you. Forgive us for overlooking the creative spirit that dwells in each of us. May we reflect you, our Creator, today as we use our hearts and hands in service to you. Draw out our hidden talents, Lord, and may we encourage one another to use our gifts in service to you. May you shine through, Light of the World, in everything we say and do. We ask your blessing upon the works of our hands. Amen.

Closing Song: "For the Beauty of the Earth," "Indescribable" (Tomlin), or "Amazed" (Anderson)

Faith Stations

Station 1. Visual Arts

What You'll Need:

Volunteers: station hosts and station assistants
Banner supplies (3 purple or blue, 1 pink and 1 white felt background approximately 42" wide by 72" long, assorted felt for decoration/lettering, fabric glue, glitter fabric paint, buttons/sequins/trim for decoration, 48" dowel rods for hanging banners, hot glue gun and glue sticks, photocopies of the lectionary readings for Advent, Bibles)
Additional felt rectangles for optional take-home banners

Directions

The station host should welcome participants and explain the three activity options, inviting them to begin with the one that most interests them. Participants can stay in this station the entire time or move to the Musical Arts or Dramatic Arts stations as desired.

Advent Banners

1. Ahead of time, the planning team should fold down the top edge (about 2") of each felt background and run a line of hot glue across to form a pocket for the dowel rod. Set each banner background on its own table.

2. On each worktable, set out the banner-making supplies (scissors, glue, trim items, additional felt, fabric paint, etc.). Also have available several photocopies of the lectionary readings for each week of Advent. The three purple or blue banners will be for weeks one, two, and four. The pink banner is for week three. The white banner is for Christmas.

3. The host and assistants should encourage group participation and find age-appropriate ways that young children can help decorate the banners without infringing on the work of others. One way to do this is to provide individual felt rectangles of blue, purple, pink, and white and allow people to make their own Advent banners for home use, as well as collaborate on the ones to keep at church. These personal banners can be strung with ribbon for hangers.

4. Each banner should include symbols of the week's theme (see below) and/or the related Scripture (visit lectionary.library.vanderbilt.edu for Revised Common Lectionary readings for that year or use traditional Christmas texts).

> Week 1: Hope/Prophecy/Expectation—blue/purple
>
> Week 2: Love/Bethlehem/John the Baptist—blue/purple
>
> Week 3: Joy/Shepherds/Mary—pink
>
> Week 4: Peace/Magi/Angels—blue
>
> Christmas Day: Jesus/Light of the World/Gift/Manger—white

5. An additional way to decorate the banner would be to use Chrismon designs. See online activity, "More Advent Arts to Celebrate" at www.judsonpress.com.

Station 2. Musical Arts

What You'll Need

Note: Ideally the church choir director/worship leader or a skilled church musician will be one of your station volunteers to facilitate incorporating musical creations into future worship services.

Volunteers: station host, station assistants, pianist/guitarist and/or choir director/worship leader/musician

Signs with station activity options (see below)

CD players and Christmas music CDs (secular, religious traditional, and religious contemporary music)

Photocopies of lyrics/song sheets for the Christmas songs on the CDs

Rhythm/small instruments (maracas, shakers, tambourines, bells, bongos, xylophones, etc.)

Photocopies of staff paper (can print out from the Internet)

Pencils

Colored Sculpey clay

Clay shaping tools

Bars of Ivory soap

Table knives for carving

Watercolor paints

Colored pencils

Watercolor and drawing paper

Assorted scrapbooking paper

Glue sticks

Construction paper

4 poster boards or flip chart sheets for Advent theme song lists (labeled *Hope, Love, Joy,* and *Peace*) hung up in a central area within the station

Directions

1. Ahead of time, set up this station in a large gathering space or in several adjoining classrooms and make signs with creative options on them (see below).

2. Set out CD players throughout the area(s), each one with a particular type of Christmas music (secular, religious traditional, religious contemporary).

3. Scatter a variety of art supplies throughout the listening areas.

4. Also set out musical staff paper, pencils, photocopies of Christmas song lyrics, and rhythm instruments.

5. As participants arrive, the station host should explain that music helps connect us to or experience the presence of God. This station will allow for both artistic responses to Christmas music, as well as creating original Christmas music. Those options include:

a. Visit the various listening stations scattered throughout the work area, choose an art medium, sit quietly, and listen to the music and use the selected art materials to create a drawing/sculpture in response to the music. Create a title for your work and list your name and the song(s) that inspired it.

b. Visit the various listening stations and keep track of your favorite songs. Find the Advent theme list posters and write your favorite titles under the appropriate themes (Hope, Love, Joy, Peace). *Note:* The host should give this list to the choir director/worship leader for worship planning consideration.

c. Visit the various listening stations and find a Christmas song that really speaks to you. Work alone or with a group to create movements or rhythm accompaniment for this song that could be shared in worship.

d. Using familiar tunes (hymns, praise songs, secular music) write new Advent or Christmas-theme lyrics. Or, if you're so gifted, write new lyrics to a simple melody you compose. Work with the station musician as needed.

Station 3. Dramatic Arts

What You'll Need

Volunteers: station host and station assistants (one per room/work area)

Copy of *The 12 Plays of Christmas* by Sheryl Anderson (Judson Press, 1999) and/or other Christmas drama resources

Costumes (traditional nativity robes/props, as well as other costumes your church has)

Mural paper for scenery

Markers/crayons

Assorted colors of construction paper

Glue sticks

Bibles

Concordances

Photocopies of lectionary readings for Advent (visit lectionary.library.vanderbilt.edu)

Notebook paper

Pens

Optional: video equipment (camera[s], blank DVDs, tripod[s]), TV with playback cables)

Directions

1. Optional: Ahead of time, recruit volunteers to bring their handheld video cameras and tripods to this event and allow them to be used by adult participants or older youth with adult supervision. *Note:* The planning team should also recruit a volunteer to edit the videos and load them on a DVD that can be shown in worship or during fellowship time before or after church.

2. Set up in a large gathering area or in adjoining classrooms so there is enough room for groups to break into smaller teams and work on multiple projects.

3. One room/space can be designated the quiet writing room for those who wish to create Advent prayers, meditations, litanies, or poems. Set out the Bibles, lectionary readings list, paper, pens, and concordances in this area.

4. In another area, place the drama/skit books, costumes, scenery making supplies (mural paper, construction paper, glue sticks, markers/crayons), and video equipment/volunteers.

5. The host should welcome participants and explain that the written and spoken word helps connect us to God. In this station, participants will have the option of creating their own Advent prayers, poems, or readings or selecting/creating a drama to perform and record.

6. Station assistants can encourage participants who prefer to work "behind the scenes" to help with scenery, wardrobe/props, or the optional video recording so that all participants feel included.

7. The host should move between the writing room and the drama room and assist/encourage as needed.

8. The host should make a list of all selected dramas and their casts and pass the list on to the pastor or worship leader for possible inclusion in future Advent services.

CHAPTER 15

A Service "Advent"ure

Key Verse: "For even the Son of Man did not come to be served, but to serve, and to give his life a ransom for many" (Mark 10:45, NRSV).

Purpose:

a. To help people refocus on worshipping Jesus during Advent

b. To offer multiple opportunities for congregation members to go out and serve in Jesus' name through one organized event

c. To issue the Advent Conspiracy congregational challenge: "Worship fully, spend less, give more, love all" (adventconspiracy.org)

Need-to-Know for Leaders

1. Based on the four key values of the Advent Conspiracy challenge, this Service "Advent"ure offers multiple ways to engage your congregation during Advent. The planning team should carefully pick and choose one or more activities that will challenge your members during a single daylong event or throughout all four weeks of Advent. Do what works best for your congregation to actively engage them in worshipping Jesus this season.

2. If you plan to offer service opportunities, start to line these up 4 to 8 weeks ahead of time. Try to get a variety of things that will engage a range of ages and abilities and offer help within your church, your community, and beyond. Be sure to use your denominational contacts if available, along with local nonprofit organizations, to see what needs and opportunities exist. Also be aware and plan accordingly if certain projects require additional materials or an advance sign-up to participate.

3. If issuing your congregation the official Advent Conspiracy challenge, be sure to visit their website (adventconspiracy.org) by mid-October to order any resource materials (promotional documents, small-group books, DVDs) you will need. Your church may choose to spread out the service opportunities throughout Advent and/or focus on a different goal of the Advent Conspiracy movement each week. (See explanation on page 70 and sample program ideas that follow.)

Note

This program is based on the four key values of a movement called Advent Conspiracy (advent conspiracy.org). Started in 2006 by five pastors as a way to spur their congregations to rethink the Christmas season, the goal of Advent Conspiracy was to help people simply worship Jesus, said national director Ken Weigel. At the heart of that goal was the question: What if Christmas became a world-changing event again?

To help people process that potentially life-changing question, the pastors focused on four key values: *worship fully, spend less, give more, and love all.* How congregations live out those values is up to them, and many churches, as well as individuals, have shared their stories on the Advent Conspiracy website. In addition, the organizers have written a simple curriculum, also available through the website, so your planning team has access to many innovative ideas in addition to the ones detailed here. However, Ken Weigel clarifies that the primary focus of Advent Conspiracy is worshiping Jesus, not creating more "stuff" to do during Advent.

The bottom line is that Advent Conspiracy hopes to help people to "be transformed by the renewing of your mind" (Romans 12:2a, NIV) and "to offer your bodies as a living sacrifice, holy and pleasing to God—this is your true and proper worship" (Romans 12:1, NIV). The planning team should be in prayer about any Advent programming that it puts in place during this season. Weigh the value of connecting people to Jesus through additional programs or services against the cost of adding to people's schedules. Above all, ask for God's guidance and do what works for your congregation, keeping in mind that Advent Conspiracy's philosophy is that simple is better and that you don't have to "do it all."

Value 1/Week 1 Focus: Worship Fully

"Advent"ure 1: Bring a simple worship service of traditional carols and Christmas Scriptures out into the world—for example, nursing homes, hospitals, prisons, veterans homes, senior housing apartment complexes, malls, and shopping centers.

What You'll Need

Volunteers: worship leader/musicians, worship team members (singers and mimes), kitchen crew (optional)

Hymnals or photocopies of song sheets with song/carol lyrics

Bible

Biblical costumes (fur tunic for John the Baptist; angel wings/halo; robes for Mary, Elizabeth, and Joseph; shepherd robes; shepherd crooks; magi robes/crowns/gifts)

Photocopies or PowerPoint of order of worship

Advent wreath, candles, and matches or lighter (optional)

Christmas cards with service times insert for guest worshippers

Advent Conspiracy printed resource materials if using and/or distributing

Refreshments (optional)

Directions

1. Recruit worship leader(s) and/or guitar player(s) (need a portable instrument).

2. Recruit worship team(s) who are willing to sing the carols loud and strong, as well as read the Scripture passages (youth will work well here if they are willing to sing and speak out). Another way to make the verses come alive is to have other volunteers wear traditional Christmas pageant costumes and pantomime actions while the verses are read. If choosing this option, the readers and the mimes should practice before leading the service. The planning team may also want

Contemporary in Context?

The planning team might also research other potential venues and create more contemporary services to fit the context, such as:

a) A children- or youth-led service for a day-care center or children's hospital. Church children can dress in costume and act out the Scripture. Bring extra animal costumes so that worshippers can also participate.

b) A coffee house–style Christmas service at a local coffee shop or mall food court with an acoustic guitar player or percussionist providing up-tempo versions of classic carols and the Christmas Scripture interpreted like a poetry reading set to music.

to recruit additional volunteers to accompany the worship leaders and sit with the guests at the host site(s).

3. In advance, identify locations willing to host your portable worship service.

4. If needed, create a schedule of which team(s) are leading worship where.

5. Ahead of time, decide if your worship leaders will also bring a "gift," maybe a Christmas card with an insert welcoming people to your church and listing service times and opportunities to connect in ministry and mission (see Love All gift idea in this chapter).

6. Make photocopies of the order of worship and any carol lyrics for the worship team(s) to bring to the service, along with directions or contact information for the host site(s). If using costumes/props for volunteers and/or an Advent wreath, pack up the costumes, props, wreath, candles, and matches or lighter.

7. Gather the worship team(s) at church before they go out to their host sites and pray with them that their offering of worship leadership will draw people closer to God and encourage them to think about his gift of love to this world.

8. Send them out!

9. If providing refreshments for worship teams back at church, plan supplies accordingly and recruit a kitchen team to handle setup and serving.

Sample Order of Worship

Welcome and Introduction of Church/Worship Team, Invitation to Worship

Lighting of the First Advent Candle: the candle of hope

Opening Carol: "O Come, All Ye Faithful," verse 1

Reading 1: Isaiah 9:2-7 (may want to use *The Message* or New Living Translation)

Responsive Carol: "O Come, O Come, Emmanuel," verses 1 and 3

Reading 2: Mark 1:1-8 (John the Baptist can appear in costume here)

Lighting of the Second Advent Candle: the candle of love

Reading 3: Luke 1:26-38 (Mary and Gabriel can appear in costume here)

Responsive Carol: "O Little Town of Bethlehem," verses 1 and 5

Reading 4: Luke 1:39-56 (Mary and Elizabeth can appear in costume here)

Lighting of the Third Advent Candle: the candle of joy

Reading 5: Luke 2:1-7 (Mary and Joseph can appear in costume here)

Responsive Carol: "Away in a Manger," verses 1 and 3

Reading 6: Luke 2:8-20 (shepherds and angels can appear in costume here)

Responsive Carol: "Hark! the Herald Angels Sing," verses 1 and 3

Lighting of the Fourth Advent Candle: the candle of peace

Get Creative?

Consider using contemporary costumes for the biblical characters, such as grunge-look clothes for John the Baptist; sequined or lamé fabric for the angels; simple, everyday clothing for Mary, Elizabeth, and Joseph such as jeans and t-shirts; overalls and flannel shirts or other work clothes for the shepherds; power suits for the magi.

Carol of Preparation: "We Three Kings of Orient Are," verse 1 and chorus

Reading 7: Matthew 2:1-12 (three magi appear in costume here)

Responsive Carol: "Silent Night," verses 1–3

Prayers of Hope, Joy, Love, and Peace (worship leader to lead)

Sending Song: "Joy to the World," verses 1 and 4

Value 2/Week 2 Focus: Spend Less

"Advent"ure 2: Create a personal Christmas budget and encourage people to reduce it overall by 10 percent and to take an additional 10 percent or more and donate it to Living Water International (Advent Conspiracy's designated charity) or a designated church Advent mission project.

What You'll Need

Photocopies of Spend Less—Gift Refocusing Worksheet (see reproducible sample in appendix)
Pencils

Directions

1. Ahead of time, create a worksheet (or use reproducible sample in appendix) with line items for various holiday expenses with a grand total, followed by lines for deductions.

2. Distribute the worksheet either when people register in advance or when they sign in on the day of the service event.

3. Optional: Set a donation goal for Advent Conspiracy's Living Water International fund or another church-chosen mission project, and make a poster illustrating the starting point, goal, and progress made along the way. Display the poster in a high traffic area of your church.

4. Continue to remind people to "spend less" during this Christmas season with weekly e-mail/bulletin/mail slot reminders, as well as pastoral encouragement during weekend services. Encourage people to share examples of how they are spending less this year, and publicize those in your reminders.

Note: If reducing Christmas expenses by 10 percent in one year seems like an overwhelming challenge to give your congregation, instead ask them to give one less

purchased gift and replace the present with the gift of presence. For more ideas on relational giving, visit rethinkingchristmas.com. Or ask congregation members to give up one category on their gift-giving list and instead write a personal note to each person in that group of recipients.

"Advent"ure 3: Organize and run a new/nearly new/eco-friendly gift exchange for the congregation and larger community, encouraging people to make holiday gift selections from the merchandise.

What You'll Need

Volunteers: donation sorters, processors, pricers, and cashiers; setup and cleanup crew; gift wrappers
Self-stick Christmas gift tags
Wrapping paper and/or holiday gift bags
Tip jar
Cash box with seed money for sale day
Advent Conspiracy printed resource materials, if using and/or distributing, or information about your designated church mission project to which the funds will go

Directions

1. Starting in August or September, seek donations of new or nearly new items from your congregation and/or community. Also consider collecting small- to medium-size boxes (shoe boxes, shirt boxes, etc.) and good condition gift bags for wrapping shoppers' purchases.

2. Organize work days for volunteers to sort, wash, sanitize, wipe down, and iron donations as needed. Make a pile of items that are beyond "nearly new" and that can be given to an area resale shop or charity. Begin to sort items by category: household, toys, women's, men's, sporting goods, etc.

3. Try a "minimum suggested donation" pricing policy. Sort donations into price categories of $1, $2, $5, etc., with those amounts being the minimum suggested donations for the items in that group.

4. Advertise the upcoming gift exchange in local papers and/or create flyers to post in area businesses or distribute to neighbors of the church, as well as to coworkers, friends, and family members. Advertise at four weeks out and again one week before (newspapers typically need a seven- to ten-day lead time for publicity). Use your local cable channel community update forum if possible. Recruit artists from the congregation to make posters to hang up around church in advance and at the exchange explaining Advent Conspiracy and the spend-less challenge.

5. Your church may also choose to have a group of volunteers available to wrap purchases (may need to purchase new holiday wrapping paper but can use donated gift bags and boxes). Have self-stick gift tags available for the purchaser.

6. Keep a tip jar handy by the wrapping station with information about Advent Conspiracy, Living Water International, or the church-chosen mission project. All tips can go to the mission fund.

7. In addition, your church may choose to offer concessions or a sloppy joe/hot dog lunch for a separate fee/donation during this event, with proceeds going to the designated mission project. Be sure to recruit enough kitchen volunteers to staff this option if selected.

Value 3/Week 3 Focus: Give More

Starting at least four to eight weeks in advance, research and confirm multiple service opportunities to engage your congregation in a day of "giving more" (of themselves, not of stuff) during week three of Advent. For each opportunity, make sure to identify a site contact person; the site location, directions, and phone number; the project time frame; the number of volunteers needed; any supplies required; and whether advance sign up is needed. Visit adventconspiracy .org/story to see what other churches, organizations, and individuals have done, or use the following ideas.

"Advent"ure 4: Serve as Salvation Army bell ringers. This is a great intergenerational opportunity as volunteers of all ages are welcome. Those under sixteen need parental permission; those under fourteen need adult supervision. Teams of no more than two to three ringers are recommended so as not to intimidate donors. To find your local Salvation Army chapter, visit salvationarmyusa.org/usn/www_usn_2.nsf and click on Ways to Give then on Volunteer. You can enter your zip code to see a list of area chapters. For a list of Frequently Asked Questions and the history of the Red Kettle Bell Ringers, visit thesalarmy.org/chris/bellringing.htm.

What You'll Need

Volunteers: bell ringers, kitchen crew (optional)
Refreshments
Paper goods

Directions

1. Create a master schedule of ringers and locations.

2. Call or e-mail volunteers as needed before service day.

3. *Optional:* Provide refreshments for ringers before or after their shift back at church. Recruit a kitchen crew and purchase supplies as needed.

"Advent"ure 5: Provide yard cleanup and/or holiday decorating assistance to members of your congregation and/or community in need of help.

What You'll Need

Volunteers: project leader for each home, workers
    for each home
Optional: evergreen wreath with card (see below)
    for each homeowner

Directions

1. Ahead of time, determine if there are older adults, single parents, or physically challenged adults in your congregation or community who need help cutting back plants, raking late-falling leaves, weather stripping doors, winterizing windows, etc. Your volunteer crews may also inquire if the homeowner would like help pulling out and/or setting up holiday decorations, outside and/or inside.

2. If your budget allows, provide the homeowners with simple evergreen wreaths for their front doors. Include a Christmas card that says: "Like this evergreen wreath, God's love for you is ever new, ever fresh. We celebrate that truth each Christmas and remember that God loved us so much that he sent his only Son to us, and whoever believes in him will live forever in God's heavenly house. We hope you will join us at God's earthly house this Christmas season at (service location, dates, and times)."

Note: Some of your volunteers may simply give the gift of presence and visit with the homeowner(s) while the work is being done.

"Advent"ure 6: Provide child care for volunteers. (If not already cleared for service by your church, the planning team will need to do the necessary criminal and child-abuse background checks before allowing volunteers to serve as child-care workers.) While the planning team is hopefully able to find intergenerational service opportunities, some situations may not be suitable for babies, toddlers, or even preschoolers. Consider recruiting a team of older adults (who love little kids) and high energy middle school students to staff a childcare room at the church for part or all of your work day. Providing this service does two things: it offers another way for older and younger congregation members to serve together, and it allows parents with small children to volunteer worry-free.

What You'll Need

Volunteers: adult and youth childcare workers
Registration form

Directions

1. Try to do advance sign-up for this service so that you know approximately how many childcare workers to provide and for how long. Length will depend on number and type of work projects offered.

2. Create a welcoming space with age-appropriate toys, snacks, music, DVDs, games, etc.

3. Supply a registration form for each child with parent cell phone numbers, emergency contact name and numbers, and any allergies, medications, and special needs noted.

4. Schedule your childcare workers in shifts so that they don't get overtired.

Do It Yourself!

Instead of using a predesigned, preprinted card, invite your participants to make the cards that will be distributed to the community. Supplies might include Christmas wrapping paper or old holiday cards from which to cut pictures to glue onto the new card. Include preprinted self-stick labels with Christmas worship service times and church contact information. Copies of the Christmas story from Luke may be taped or glued into the card.

Value 4/Week 4 Focus: Love All

"Advent"ure 7: Create a simple Christmas card and gift to distribute in the neighborhood, in the community, in local businesses, and to friends, coworkers, and family members that will share the message of God's love and invite people to join you during Advent (and beyond) to celebrate God's gift to the world.

What You'll Need

Volunteers: artist to design the card two months ahead of time, project leader for service work day, card assemblers, card distributors
Photocopies of a preprinted Christmas card tailored to your church (see description below and sample in this chapter)
Candy canes, 1 per card if using sample idea in this chapter
Optional: Supplies for creating hand-made Christmas cards (construction paper or cardstock, markers, crayons, colored pencils, holiday-theme stickers or foam shape stickers, Christmas wrapping paper or old Christmas cards, scissors, glue sticks, etc.)

Directions

1. Six to eight weeks in advance, recruit a volunteer to design a two-sided church Christmas postcard. One side will list all regular and special Christmas worship service times, as well as church contact information. The other side will share your message of God's love. See the sample in the appendix, which can be adapted as needed for your congregation and community.

2. Host a work session during the last weekend of Advent where participants can attach the candy canes to the cards and create distribution routes for volunteers to go into the community and pass out the cards. Plan to have extras for volunteers to take into their own neighborhoods and workplaces.

Note: Your church may want to make these cards available earlier in Advent to pass out during your movable worship services or during your service projects or to have on hand for congregation members to distribute on their own. Plan accordingly if you want to use them before week four. This may include editing the text to list other Advent programming or special services.

CHAPTER 16

Jesus, Light of the World: A Luminary Crosswalk

Need-to-Know for Leaders

1. This intergenerational program requires a large indoor space for forming a cross out of people and, later, luminaries. For the most visual impact, it would be better to offer this program in the midafternoon or later, so that the luminaries really light up the darkness, but it can be done during the day. The planning team also has the option of forming the final luminary cross outside if that works for your congregation. The outside piece would take an additional 15 minutes or so.

2. The planning team should coordinate with your building team or custodian so that you are aware of local fire codes and fire safety issues since this program involves many candles. If lighting the candles inside and/or if you expect a high child to adult ratio (more children than adults), you may need to switch to battery-operated tea lights (available online for approximately $.85/piece; search "battery operated tea light"). If you use real candles, be sure to have fire extinguishers and buckets of water on hand, just in case of emergency.

3. For a shorter program, serve refreshments during the opening gathering and work time and omit the closing fellowship component.

Sample Schedule

3:00–3:40	Gathering Time and Station 1 (indoors)
3:40–4:10	Station 2 (indoors, with optional 15 minutes outdoors)
4:10–4:30	Fellowship (indoors)

Key Verse: "The people who walk in darkness will see a great light. For those who live in a land of deep darkness, a light will shine" (Isaiah 9:2, NLT).

Purpose:

a. To reflect on Jesus as the Light of the World

b. To create quiet time in the midst of Christmas craziness

c. To experience walking in darkness and seeing light shine

Faith Stations

Station 1. Preparing to Walk in the Light

What You'll Need

Volunteers: greeter/registrar, station host, setup and
cleanup crew

Newspaper or other table coverings for worktables

Markers

Scissors

Cellophane (multiple colors)

Black permanent markers

Glue sticks

12" high white paper bags (heavy duty restaurant
quality, 1 per person)

Play sand (figure 1.5 pounds/luminary which will
be about 4 cups)

Small votive or tea light candles (1/luminary, can
also use battery-operated tea lights found online
for approximately $.85/light, search "battery operated
tea light")

Christmas music / player

Directions

1. Ahead of time, set up worktables and cover with
newspaper or inexpensive plastic tablecloths. Set out
the white paper bags, scissors, markers, cellophane,
and glue sticks. Have Christmas music playing during
the work time.

Note: You could choose to serve refreshments during this gathering/work time and simply end the
evening with the luminary lighting.

2. As people check in, the station host should welcome them and invite them to come to the worktables.
The host should tell people that they can write their
names on the bottom of the bags; however, they are invited to leave their luminaries at church for use on
Christmas Eve instead of taking them home at the end
of the program.

3. Participants can decorate their luminaries using
markers to draw a scene from the Christmas story, cutting out a snowflake-type pattern in the middle of the
bag (approximately 6" from the bottom), or creating
a stained glass effect by cutting a 3" x 5" rectangle out
of the front and back of the bag about halfway up. Cut
two 4" x 6" sheets of cellophane to cover the holes.
For a fancier stained glass look, cut smaller pieces of
other colors of cellophane and lightly glue them to the
rectangle piece or use black permanent marker to
draw a design on the cellophane rectangle. Glue the
rectangle onto the inside of the bag over each hole.

Note: The planning team should make a few sample luminaries using different decorating techniques
and set them out to guide participants.

4. After the bags are designed, fill the bottom of
each bag with 3–4" inches of sand (approximately 4
cups). Work over a plastic tablecloth so that spilled
sand can be easily cleaned up.

5. Next, place a tea light in the bottom of the bag,
twisting it down about ½" into the sand to secure it.

6. Planning team should line up all the completed
luminaries on a table so that they are easily picked up
by the volunteers for the final step of Station 2.

Station 2. Walking in Darkness and Light

What You'll Need

Volunteer: station host, worship leader and/or guitar/
piano player

1 flashlight

4 Bibles

Photocopies of song lyrics for "Thy Word" (Grant)

Recording of "Thy Word" and MP3 or CD player if no
guitar/piano player

Participant-made luminaries from Station 1

Long wooden kitchen matches (4" or longer) or butane
taper lighters

Fire extinguishers and buckets of water in case of fire

Chairs for people who can't stand for prolonged
periods

Directions

1. If possible, darken the windows and turn off some
of the lights in the space you are using so that it's dim
but people can still read the song sheet.

2. The station host should gather participants in a
circle. Provide chairs for those who need to sit. Distribute copies of the song lyrics for "Thy Word." Pass
out Bibles to 3 volunteer readers. Mark passages for
them ahead of time: Mark 1:1-3; Proverbs 6:23; Isaiah 9:2,6-7.

3. The host holds up the Bible and says: *The Word of God for the people of God.* (Participants may respond "Thanks be to God" if that is part of your faith tradition.)

4. The host holds up the flashlight, turns it on, shines it around circle and says: *God's Word is a lamp for our feet and a light for our path. Those who are able, please follow me as we sing "Thy Word."* (Host is going to move people into two lines that form a cross.)

5. Worship leader starts the singing while the host takes the hand/arm of a person to form the beginning of a line, which will become the long piece of a cross running the length of your indoor space. Planning team members should assist any seated participants in moving their chairs to become part of the cross.

6. As the singing continues, the host will create a second line, leading them into position as the arms of the cross. The worship leader should watch the progress and repeat the verses/chorus as needed until the cross is formed.

7. After singing, the host says to group: *God's Word is a light for our path, but Jesus is the Light of the World. Hear what John the Baptist said about Jesus coming to us here on earth.*

8. Reader reads the Mark passage.

9. Host says: *People of God, are you making your paths straight so that you can follow where the Light of the World leads? Hear what Scripture says about God's Word in Proverbs 6:23.*

10. Reader reads the Proverbs passage.

11. Host says: *People of God, God has planned our way from the beginning of time to the end. God's Word tells us how to live and where to go, and God's Son leads the way. God makes it easy to follow Jesus, and yet time and time again, we turn away, bound and determined to forge our own path. Hear these words of Isaiah, written hundreds of years before Jesus' birth, yet still relevant for us today.*

12. Reader reads the Isaiah passage.

13. Host says: *God sent the Son into the darkness of our broken world that first Christmas to be the Light of the World. We are going to close our worship time by forming a cross with our luminaries and singing "This Little Light of Mine." Please quietly pick up a luminary—any one will do right now—and reform a circle.*

14. Allow participants to pick up a luminary and reform a circle. After people are in place, a planning team member should turn off the lights. (*Optional:* the planning team may choose to take the group outside for the final cross formation, Scripture, and singing. The directions remain the same, although if the group moves outside, people have the freedom to remain in the light of cross for individual meditation time after the program ends. Planning team members should monitor the outdoor setting if people choose to stay and pray, and be sure that all candles are extinguished before the last person goes back inside.)

15. Host says: *In a moment, we will make a cross out of our luminaries and light their candles, as a sign that we welcome the Light of the World into our hearts, into our lives, not only now during Advent, but every day until he comes again. Hear these words from his faithful disciple, and see how the light shines in the darkness. Know that the darkness has not, cannot, will not ever overcome. . . . "In the beginning was the Word, and the Word was with God, and the Word was God. He was with God in the beginning. Through him all things were made; without him nothing was made that has been made. In him was life, and that life was the light of all people. The light shines in the darkness, and the darkness has not overcome it"* (John 1:1-5, TNIV).

16. Host and planning team direct people to begin setting down their luminaries in two lines to make a cross.

17. The worship leader should start people quietly singing "This Little Light of Mine" as the planning team lights the tea lights. After the candles are all lit, the worship leader should continue the singing with at least one of the following and invite people to join in: "It Came upon the Midnight Clear," "O Holy Night," "Silent Night," "Be Thou My Vision," "Break Forth, O Beauteous Heavenly Light," "Here I Am to Worship" (Hughes), or "Shine, Jesus, Shine" (Kendrick).

18. When the worship leader ends the singing, the host says: *People of God, say these words with me: The light shines in the darkness* (people echo) *and the darkness has not overcome it* (people echo). *Amen* (people echo). *Go out into the world and be lights that shine for Christ. Go in peace.*

19. Be sure to extinguish all candles and safely store the luminaries for use on Christmas Eve before leaving church grounds for the night.

Fellowship

What You'll Need

Volunteers: kitchen crew

Refreshments (warm beverages and light-themed snacks, such as star or candle cutout cookies)

Paper goods

Directions

1. Participants can move to the gathering area for fellowship and refreshments.

2. The planning team should make sure all candles are extinguished and luminaries are moved out of the way if the fellowship is taking place in the same space.

CHAPTER 17

The Twelve Days of Christmas and the Never-Ending Story

Key Verse: "'I am the Alpha and the Omega—the beginning and the end,' says the Lord God. 'I am the one who is, who always was, and who is still to come—the Almighty One'" (Revelation 1:8, NLT).

Purpose:

a. To introduce the historical significance of the 12 days of Christmas, connecting Christmas to Epiphany

b. To connect a somewhat secular Christmas song with Christian theology

c. To prepare to celebrate the hope, love, joy, and peace of Christmas even after the climax of Christmas Day

Leader Need-to-Know

1. This intergenerational faith and fellowship event centers around the lyrics of the Christmas carol "The Twelve Days of Christmas." Scholars and amateur historians alike have debated whether this song features Christian symbolism that was used as a "hidden code" for English Catholics to learn the tenets of their faith after King Henry VIII severed ties with the Catholic Church in Rome in 1534, creating the Church of England. Urban legend research site www.snopes.com says that there is no positive proof that this song has religious roots. Whether it is merely a legend, like so many others, or a true story whose documentation has been lost over time, the lyrics of "The Twelve Days of Christmas" connect nicely with important symbols and symbolic numbers in Jewish and Christian traditions alike. Therefore, in the spirit of wisdom and truth, Christians might choose to view the song through the lens of Scripture and explore its creative symbolism and its connection to faith without acknowledging the song as a historically significant piece of religious music. The bottom line, then, for your planning team is to consider the theological values of your church and decide whether this program will help or hinder the faith development of your congregation.

2. This event features one main station in the format of an all-ages game show that all participants play at one time. It does provide a second, optional hands-on craft project, which can be done in the gathering area so that participants can work on it or move directly into the fellowship time after worship.

3. For a shorter program, serve refreshments during the opening gathering time and omit the Twelve Days of Christmas Cartons activity.

Sample Schedule

2:50–3:15   Registration/Gathering Time
3:15–4:15   Game Show Station
4:15–4:30   Worship
4:30–5:00   Twelve Days of Christmas Cartons
                 (see below for description and
                 instructions)/Fellowship

Faith Stations

Station 1. Twelve Days of Christmas Trivia

What You'll Need

Volunteers: greeters, game show host, setup and
   cleanup crew
Card or board games
Art supplies
Christmas music / player
Flip chart and markers
Podium (with microphone if possible)
Text of "The Twelve Days of Christmas" with list
   of Christian symbols for host (see appendix)
Photocopies or PowerPoint of "The Twelve Days
   of Christmas" lyrics
Optional: prizes for winning team and/or all par-
   ticipants

Directions

1. Ahead of time in a large meeting area, set up groups of six to eight chairs, based on the total number of people expected.

2. Place a Bible in each group.

3. At the front of the room, set up the flip chart and a podium for the host. If you have a space with a stage available, place the host and the host's equipment on the stage.

4. At the other end of the meeting room, set up a registration table. As people check in, assign them to teams of six to eight people of mixed ages. Families can stay together but should be intentionally paired with single adults, couples, and/or seniors.

5. Play Christmas music (but not "The Twelve Days of Christmas") and provide simple card or board games or art supplies to keep children busy until the game show starts.

6. When all participants have arrived, the host asks them to sit by teams in the groups of chairs. The host should then introduce the game show, briefly summarize the historical debate concerning the song (as noted on page 79) and explain that the group will not be arguing whether the legend is fact or fiction. Instead, participants will use the song's words and symbols to explore the Christian faith.

7. To begin play, the host selects a volunteer to be the first actor/artist (e.g., the person with the birthday closest to Christmas).

8. The host will award points for correct answers in each of these categories: Lovely Lyrics, Secret Symbols, and Bible Basics. You can award prizes to the team(s) with the most points at the end of the game. Game rules are described below.

Twelve Days of Christmas Trivia Game Show Rules

1. Divide participants into teams of six to eight players.

2. Select a volunteer to be the first actor/artist.

3. Remind teams to discuss possible answers quietly among themselves and raise their hands to answer. Teams shouting out answers will be disqualified from responding to that question.

4. The host reads from the song lyrics, "On the first day of Christmas, my true love gave to me," and ask the volunteer to pantomime the first object given. (The host may show the end of the line if the volunteer doesn't know what the true love gave.)

5. Ask teams to guess.

6. If no one guesses correctly, ask the volunteer to draw the object. The artist can use picture clues instead of drawing the object itself (i.e., for turtledove, draw a turtle + a dove). The host can give hints to the actor/artist as needed.

7. Award a point in the category of Lovely Lyrics to the team guessing correctly.

8. Now ask the teams if they can guess what the creative Christian symbolism is for that object. The host may tell teams that the symbols all represent key pieces of the Christian faith, mainly taken from the Bible. The host may give hints if teams are unable to guess correctly (e.g., The partridge in a pear tree represents the single most important piece of our faith. Answer: Jesus).

9. Award a point in the category of Secret Symbols for the correct answer.

10. Now read the Scripture citation (book, chapter, and verse) that goes along with the symbol. The first team to find the verse and raise their hands gets a point. Ask the winning team to read the verse out loud.

11. Award a point in the category of Bible Basics for the correct answer.

12. Continue this process through all 12 objects in the song. Total up the team points and award prizes at the end of the game show.

Worship

What You'll Need

Volunteers: worship leader/musician, one reader

Photocopies or PowerPoint of "The Twelve Days of Christmas" lyrics

Photocopies or PowerPoint of order of worship

Bible

Copy of *The 12 Days of Christmas: The Story behind a Favorite Christmas Song* by Helen Haidle (Zonderkidz, 2003) or other similar picture book about the song

Directions

1. The worship leader/musician can take the host's place on stage and lead the group in singing "The Twelve Days of Christmas" and then proceed with the rest of the service.

2. Depending on the size of your crowd, the reader can hold up the book to show the pictures, or if your congregation uses PowerPoint, consider scanning the pictures and showing them on a screen as the story is read.

Order of Worship

Opening Song: "The Twelve Days of Christmas"

Responsive Reading (from Revelation 1:8, NLT):

Leader: I am the Alpha and the Omega, says the Lord God.

People: You are the Hero in our never-ending story!

Leader: I am the beginning and the end, says the Lord.

People: You know the story of our lives, from our first breaths to our last.

Leader: I am the one who is.

People: You are Emmanuel, God with us.

Leader: I am the one who always was.

People: In the beginning, you created the heavens and the earth. In the beginning was the Word, and the Word was with God and the Word was God.

Leader: I am the one who is still to come.

All: You are the Almighty One, Lord Jesus, Wonderful Counselor, Mighty God, Everlasting Father, Prince of Peace, the Living Word, Author of our never-ending story. To you be all glory and honor, forever and ever.

Meditation: Leader reads *The 12 Days of Christmas: The Story behind a Favorite Christmas Song* or other similar book.

Closing Song: "Joy to the World" or "Revelation Song" (Riddle)

Station 2. Twelve Days of Christmas Cartons

Note: All participants go to Station 1 and worship together. They will then have the option of going to Station 2 following worship. If participants do not want to make a Twelve Days of Christmas Carton, they may either leave or stay in the gathering area if the planning team wants to offer refreshments for a fellowship time.

What You'll Need

Photocopies of Twelve Days of Christmas Carton directions (see appendix)

Empty cardboard egg cartons (1 per household and/or per child, depending on planning team decision)

12 white plastic Easter eggs per carton (available online from party or novelty supply companies)

4.25" x 3.6" slips of paper (12 slips per carton, equivalent to 2 pieces of 8.5" x 11" divided into 6 sections each; could be construction or copy paper, white or colored)

12 days of Christmas stickers (ordered from online company [search "12 Days of Christmas stickers"] or copies of reproducible 12 Days of Christmas free online clip art [search "12 Days of Christmas clip art])

Christmas wrapping paper for decorating cartons

Markers, crayons, colored pencils
Tape
Glue sticks
Permanent markers
Egg decorating supplies: self-adhesive holiday foam
  shapes, self-adhesive jewels, ribbon, etc.

Directions

1. Depending on your program space, you can set up the worktables in the same area as the game show, but cover the supplies with a cloth so that people don't "cheat" and use the materials as hints for the game show. Or you can set this activity up in a separate room.

2. The Twelve Days of Christmas Cartons follow the song's 12 objects and include the key Bible verses that can connect to each item. One egg from the carton can be opened and the Bible verse read on each of the 12 days of Christmas from December 26 to January 5.

3. Ahead of time, print out sheets of self-stick labels with the song object and Bible verse listed together for each of the 12 objects in the song (e.g., the stickers on the first sheet would all say *partridge in a pear tree/Matthew 23:37*, the second sheet would say *two turtledoves/2 Timothy 3:14-17*).

4. Make copies of 12 Days of Christmas clip art found online or order 12 Days of Christmas stickers. If necessary, shrink the clip art on the copier so that it can be cut and glued to the 4.25" x 3.6" papers.

5. Make 12 piles on the supply table from the 12 object/verse sticker copies and the 12 Days of Christmas clip art or prepurchased stickers.

6. The slips of paper, drawing supplies, tape, and glue sticks can go in a common area, along with the wrapping paper and permanent markers for decorating the egg cartons and/or eggshells.

7. Make photocopies of the instructions (see appendix) and set out with the supplies.

8. This is a self-serve activity, so just set out all the materials and instruction sheets (one per household recommended, although the planning team may want to provide enough so that each child in a household can make a set). Participants will put them together assembly-line style.

9. Also set out a worktable or two with decorating materials so that if participants want to decorate their individual eggs or their cartons, they can do so.

Fellowship

What You'll Need

Refreshments
Paper goods
Kitchen crew

Directions

1. If serving refreshments after the game show, recruit a kitchen crew and purchase necessary supplies.

2. Snack options might include pear slices, cutout cookies shaped as various birds (dove, songbird, swan, hen) or musical instruments (drums, flutes/pipes), foil-wrapped gold coin chocolates, hard-boiled eggs or deviled eggs, milk, and perhaps also a "fruit of the Spirit" platter of fresh fruits.

CHAPTER 18

The Shepherd Takes Control: Youth Drama and Worship

Key Verse: "I am the good shepherd; I know my sheep and my sheep know me" (John 10:14, NIV).

Purpose:

a. To celebrate Christmas Eve as a community of faith (all ages)

b. To understand that Jesus calls us to action in his name

c. To engender a desire to be both the good sheep who follow Jesus and the shepherds who look for the wayward and the lost in Jesus' name

Leader Need-to-Know

1. This service can be used during Advent or on Christmas Eve. It incorporates a short drama that uses youth participants, although adults can be recruited as needed.

2. The planning team may want to set up 3–5 rehearsals before the service to practice the drama.

3. For a shorter service, choose just one of the Sung Response songs to open the service, have the drama, and close with a final song and benediction.

What You'll Need

Volunteers: greeters, worship leader/musician(s)/vocalist(s), director and/or drama assistants, drama cast (approximately 16 players, see script that follows)

Simple Bible-time costumes: robes/belts for Mary, Joseph, shepherds, grown-up Jesus; a shepherd crook; tinsel garland crowns and/or white robes/wings for angels; toy sheep for junior shepherds

Hillside mural background

2 chairs for Joseph and Mary

Manger with doll

Photocopies of song sheets, hymnals, or PowerPoint with lyrics

Photocopies of scripts for participants available online at www .judsonpress.com

Optional (but very helpful): wireless handheld, lavaliere, or head-set microphones for speaking characters

Directions

1. Greeters should welcome worshippers, pass out bulletins, and invite them to be seated in the worship area.

2. Worship leader, musicians, and vocalists should provide 15 minutes of meditative music before the service begins.

3. Director should be seated up front near the cast and have a copy of the script available for prompts.

4. Drama assistants should be divided between the front and the back of the worship area so that they can cue actors as needed.

Order of Worship

Meditative Music

Call to Worship

Leader: Shout with joy to the Lord, all the earth!

People: We call out to you, Good Shepherd. Be here with us now!

Leader: Worship the Lord with gladness. Come before him, singing with joy.

People: Lord, you are the Good Shepherd. You seek us. You save us. Joyfully, joyfully, we adore you!

Leader: Acknowledge that the Lord is God! He made us, and we are his.

People: We are his people, the sheep of his pasture.

Leader: Enter his presence with thanksgiving; come before him with praise.

People: Lord, we give you thanks. We honor your holy name.

All: Lord, you are good, and your love for us surrounds us forever. You are our Good Shepherd, faithful to all generations. May we always follow you.

Sung Response: Choose one: "All People That on Earth Do Dwell," "God Is Great" (Sampson), "Shout to the Lord" (Zschech).

Old Testament Reading: Micah 5:2-5

Sung Response: Choose one: "O Come, O Come, Emmanuel," "Majesty" (Hayford), "How Great Is Our God" (Tomlin), "In Your Hands I'm So Secure" (Morgan).

Gospel Reading: John 10:1-18

Unison Prayer: Lord, God, we come to you today as sheep in need of a shepherd. Life is hard. It's easy for us to wander off. It's easy to follow the crowd. It's easy to fall prey to the wolves in the world. Save us from ourselves. Rescue us from our wandering ways. You are the Good Shepherd! We praise you and thank you that you came to earth as a baby, that you led God's people to salvation through your death on the cross, that you will bring about a new heaven and a new earth when you return to us again. Until that time, may we always follow you and share the Good News: that Jesus Christ, the Good Shepherd, lives. Amen!

Drama: *The Good Shepherd* (see script)

Closing Song: "The First Noel," "Rise Up, Shepherd, and Follow," or "As Shepherds Watched Their Flocks by Night"

The Good Shepherd

Setting: A church sanctuary/auditorium where the annual Christmas Eve pageant is taking place

Props/Costumes: robes/belts for shepherds; crook for Head Shepherd; stuffed toy sheep for Junior Shepherds; tinsel garland halos for angels; white robes and/or wings for angels; 2 chairs; manger with doll; mural backdrop of hillside with city in the distance (optional)

Cast:

Shawn (the Head Shepherd, older than Junior Shepherds by several years)

Junior Shepherds (ideally kindergarten/first grade students, at least age five)

Lead Angel

Angel Choir (4 or more)

Sunday School Teachers (at least 2 adults or teens)

Narrator

Holy Family (Mary, Joseph, manger with "baby Jesus")

Grown-up Jesus

Scene 1: Getting Ready to Follow the Leader

Tech note: Grown-up Jesus should be seated directly behind Mary's and Joseph's chairs with his back to everyone until he speaks at the end. Mary and Joseph will enter the worship area from the back, walk down the center aisle, and be seated at the back right of the stage. The angels should be ready to enter the worship area down the center aisle from the back, as well. The shepherds should be off to the right side of the stage but still in front where they can be seen. They should appear to be in the final stages of getting ready for their entrance—putting on their robes, teachers helping to tie robes and handing sheep to the Junior Shepherds.

Teacher 1: Okay, Shawn, I think you're ready. Here's your crook *(hands crook to Shawn)*. Just lead the Junior Shepherds into church like we practiced.

Shawn: *(Nods yes.)*

Teacher 2: And you, Junior Shepherds, listen up. Remember that Shawn here is in charge. You need to follow him, okay? *(Junior Shepherds are excitedly looking around, nudging each other with their sheep, making baaing noises and generally not paying attention to Teacher 2.)*

Teacher 1: All right, shepherds, time to make your entrance. Shawn, lead them in.

Scene 2: Follow the Leader

Tech note: Teachers should assist in getting Junior Shepherds in line behind Shawn, who then slowly leads them across the front of the stage area, stopping diagonally across the stage from where the Holy Family will be seated. This movement takes place as Narrator begins speaking in Scene 2. Mary and Joseph should also begin walking up to the stage area from the back after the shepherds are in place and proceed to their seats at the back right of the stage area while Narrator is reading about their journey to Bethlehem.

As shepherds make their entrance, Junior Shepherds should begin jostling and nudging each other with their toy sheep and starting to smile and laugh a little at their own antics. Shawn should occasionally look back and shake his head no. Shawn should then herd them up to the left front corner of the stage and stand behind the group where he can see what is going on.

Narrator: At that time the Roman emperor, Augustus, decreed that a census should be taken throughout the Roman Empire. (This was the first census taken when Quirinius was governor of Syria.) All returned to their own ancestral towns to register for this census.

(Two Junior Shepherds now begin pushing each other with their sheep; Shawn gently taps them with his crook and shakes his head no.)

Narrator: *(continuing)* And because Joseph was a descendant of King David, he had to go to Bethlehem in Judea, David's ancient home. He traveled there from the village of Nazareth in Galilee. He took with him Mary, his fiancée, who was now obviously pregnant.

(Now 4 Junior Shepherds begin pushing each other with their sheep; Shawn taps them a little harder with his crook and shakes his head more forcefully no.)

Narrator: *(continuing)* And while they were there, the time came for her baby to be born. She gave birth to her first child, a son. She wrapped him snugly in strips of cloth and laid him in a manger, because there was no lodging available for them.

(All Junior Shepherds begin pushing each other with their sheep; Shawn moves into the center of them and touches each of them on the head and loudly whispers, "No!" All Junior Shepherds finally stop and look at Shawn with big, surprised eyes and nod yes several times.)

(Mary and Joseph should now be seated on stage. Angels begin their entrance from the back as Narrator continues.)

Narrator: *(continuing)* That night there were shepherds staying in the fields nearby, guarding their flocks of sheep.

(Shawn moves to center stage, and Junior Shepherds obediently fan out behind him as Angels approach.)

Narrator: Suddenly, an angel of the Lord appeared among them, and the radiance of the Lord's glory surrounded them. They were terrified.

(As Angels approach, Shawn falls to his knees and shields his face with his arms. Junior Shepherds follow his lead.)

Narrator: *(continuing)* But the angel reassured the shepherds . . .

Lead Angel: Don't be afraid! I bring you good news that will bring great joy to all people.

(Shawn puts his hands down and stares at the angel in awe. Junior Shepherds follow his lead.)

Lead Angel: *(continuing)* The Savior—yes, the Messiah, the Lord—has been born today in Bethlehem, the city of David! And you will recognize him by this sign: You will find a baby wrapped snugly in strips of cloth, lying in a manger.

Lead Angel and Angel Choir: Glory to God in highest heaven, and peace on earth to those with whom God is pleased.

(Shawn stands and claps his hands with joy or raises them up to the sky with a big smile on his face. Junior Shepherds follow his lead.)

Narrator: When the angels had returned to heaven, the shepherds said to each other . . .

Shawn: Let's go to Bethlehem! Let's see this thing that has happened, which the Lord has told us about. *(Junior Shepherds nod in agreement as Shawn is speaking.)*

Narrator: They hurried to the village and found Mary and Joseph.

(Shawn leads Junior Shepherds to Mary and Joseph and they all bow down before the manger.)

Narrator: *(continuing)* And there was the baby, lying in the manger. After seeing him, the shepherds told everyone what had happened and what the angel had said to them about this child.

Shawn and Junior Shepherds: *(walking up and down the aisles, talking to the congregation)* Did you hear the good news? God's Son was born tonight! Jesus Christ our Savior was born tonight! Praise God!

(Shepherds all move to center stage and kneel with their backs to the congregation.)

Narrator: All who heard the shepherds' story were astonished, but Mary kept all these things in her heart and thought about them often. The shepherds went back to their flocks, glorifying and praising God for all they had heard and seen. It was just as the angel had told them [Luke 2:1-20, NLT].

(Mary, Joseph, Lead Angel, and Angel Choir join the shepherds at center stage, kneeling with their backs to the congregation as Jesus stands and moves to center stage, facing them.)

Jesus: Have you heard the Good News? I am God's Son, that baby who was born in Bethlehem, that baby who brought such joy to the world. Well, guess what? The Good News still stands. I am the Good News, the Living Word, the Savior, the Messiah, Wonderful Counselor, Mighty God, Everlasting Father, Prince of Peace. Above all, I am the Good Shepherd. I know my sheep, and my sheep know me. And those who hear the Good News and obey it and then share it with the world become shepherds in my name. I say to you, the sheep are plentiful but the shepherds are few. Are you ready to join the fold and follow me?

(Jesus begins to walk out of the worship area and down the center aisle. Cast members look at one another questioningly and one by one get up and follow Jesus down the aisle.)

All Cast Members: *(to congregation as they walk)* Did you hear the Good News? The Good Shepherd lives. We live to follow the Good Shepherd.

APPENDIX

Reproducible Resources and Handouts

All handouts can be found online at www.judsonpress.com.

Room for One More

by Rachel Gilmore

The smell of sweet pine tickled Joe's nose as soon as he opened the barn door. Mom was already busy spreading shavings in one of the open stalls. "Do we have a new horse coming in?" Joe asked, tearing open the next bag for her.

"I got the call late last night," Mom said. "Chase is a nine-month-old Appaloosa whose owners are moving. They can't take him with them, not to mention he's a little ornery. Most days you literally have to chase him if you want to groom him, so they've had a hard time selling him."

Now Joe found it just plain strange that some people sell their horses like they'd sell a bed in a yard sale. Around his house, horses were family. Mom would no sooner sell Danny Boy than she'd sell Joe. And a nine-month-old—why he was just a baby.

"Joe, can you get me two buckets to hang for Chase's water and food?" Mom asked. "I've got to start feeding. I want that done before he arrives."

Heading to the storeroom, Joe could see Miss Vivian and her daughter Libby Lou wandering into the gloom of the arena from where they'd been grazing out back. Mom had raised them both from the day each was born, and they ran the barn. They expected to eat first. They expected to drink first. They pushed the others out of the way to be first to come in at night and first to go out in the morning. These two knew the routine, and they'd bite anyone who stepped out of line, horse or human, although that didn't fly with Mom. Sometimes Mom held them back and took them in last just to remind them who was the HHIC—head horse in charge!

Suddenly Joe felt the arena dirt shaking under his feet even before he heard the terrifying thunder of Libby Lou and Miss Vivian hurtling toward him. "Morning, girls," Joe shouted, standing his ground like Mom had taught him. "Whoa!" he yelled, putting his hands up in front of his chest. "Back off!" And they did, turning quickly and trotting away like they weren't really going to run him over—this time.

"Come over here, silly girls," Joe called, digging out two more peppermints and holding them in his open palms. Curious, the pair walked over, heads angled with one ear forward and one ear back. Their tricky lips snatched up the mints, and they chomped happily, leaving Joe to finally find his buckets.

"Joe? Son, what are you doing back there?" Mom's voice disappeared in the cavernous space of the arena.

"I'm coming, Mom," Joe shouted, closing the storeroom door and tromping back through the dust. Libby Lou and Miss Viv ignored him now, more interested in the hay Mom had set out for them. It was still so dim inside that Joe almost missed Lady J, who stood shyly in the corner.

"Well, good morning, Lady J. Come here, pretty girl," Joe said softly. Lady J hesitated then pranced toward him, head held high, nose tucked in, tail flouncing behind her. She could have been a carousel horse at the county fair—she was that beautiful. Lady J reached Joe and leaned her head in toward his chest, rubbing her nose under his chin and giving him a quick kiss too.

"That's a good girl," Joe whispered. "Do you like peppermints?" Lady J's head bobbed up and down—a trick Joe had taught her. She pushed against him, nosing his pockets for a treat. "Here you, go, Lady J. Last one's for you." Joe took the mint out and offered it to her. Lady J wiggled her lips and sucked it in, munching quickly and giving a minty kiss in return.

Pulling a small rubber curry comb from his back pocket, Joe carefully groomed her neck and withers. Lady J closed her eyes and dropped her head, relaxing. It had taken months of soft brushing, whispered words, and bags of treats before Lady J learned to trust her new family.

"I found her in the old Whitfield place outside of Davidson," Doc Weller had told Mom when he showed up with Lady J in his horse trailer the day before Joe's tenth birthday. "Those folks picked up and left her behind with no food or water. I thought maybe you two would have room for one more." Now, two years later, Lady J was like a puppy dog, coming when called and almost knocking people over with her not-so-ladylike kisses.

"Hey, Mom," Joe said as he handed her the buckets, "I was just wondering . . . do you think our family can ever get too big?"

"Too big?" Mom repeated slowly, shaking her head. "Joe, you know how I feel about that. In our barn, there's always room for . . ."

"One more!" Joe finished with her.

"Right!" Mom said, wrapping him up in a hay-filled hug.

For use with chapter 4, "An Advent Service of Hope," in 'Tis the Season: Church Celebrations for Advent & Christmas by Rachel Gilmore

Advent Mixer

Directions: Working on your own or with a partner, find someone who fits each statement and have that person sign his or her name by it. Return your sheet to the station host as soon as you find a person for each item.

Your name(s) _____

1. Received a bicycle for Christmas one year. _____

2. Likes hot chocolate with whipped cream, not marshmallows. _____

3. Went Christmas caroling last year. _____

4. Knows what wassail is. _____

   (Definition: _____)

5. Celebrates using another country's Christmas traditions. _____

   (Name of country: _____)

6. Received coal in his or her stocking one time. _____

7. Played the part of a shepherd in a Christmas play. _____

8. Likes candy canes better than gingerbread cookies. _____

9. Sets up a nativity scene at home before Christmas. _____

10. Uses an Advent wreath at home during Christmas. _____

11. Favorite carol is "Silent Night." _____

12. Can sing the first verse of "Away in a Manger." _____

13. Knows the name of the angel who visited Mary. _____

    (Angel's name: _____)

14. Knows what Joseph did for a living. _____

    (Joseph's job: _____)

15. Opens presents on Christmas Day, not Christmas Eve. _____

Advent Devotional Booklet
Outreach Version

What You'll Need

Scissors

Hole punchers

Yarn or ribbon for binding booklets

Photocopies of Advent devotional booklet, Outreach
version (see reproducible pages to follow or download online at www.judsonpress.com; 1 per household for giveaway, ideally with a wreath; see chapter
8 for instructions on making such a wreath)

Booklet Instructions

a. Photocopy the devotional booklet pages on
8.5 x 11-inch paper, double-sided, if you prefer.

b. Have volunteer(s) assemble the devotional
booklet pages in order.

c. Punch three holes down the side of each
assembled book.

d. Run a piece of ribbon/yarn through each
hole and tie.

e. Sign the cover page of the outreach booklet
as directed. Color the cover as desired.

An Advent Devotional

"For God so loved the world . . ." (John 3:16)

Inspired by God and prepared for you by

_____

[NAME]

We wish you a Merry Christmas! At our church, we get ready for Christmas by celebrating Advent. This is a time of preparation that begins about one month before Christmas. Just like we have family holiday traditions that we look forward to and celebrate year after year, we also have church traditions that move us toward Christmas day. Singing Christmas carols, lighting candles, and reading the Christmas story are often a part of those traditions. The Advent wreath also carries over some of those traditions from church into our homes, helping us keep the focus on Jesus during this busy season.

We have prepared this Advent wreath and readings for you and your family to use at home. Our hope is that it will bring you the gift of a little peace and quiet in the midst of the Christmas craziness out in the world. Each day you and your family can light the Advent candle(s) and read the short verse that follows. Over the next month, we hope that you might begin thinking more about what it means to you that God so loved the world that he sent his only Son to us (John 3:16). We also invite you to join us for worship or other special Advent programs over the coming weeks. We wish you a Merry Christmas!

Week One Readings

Directions: Each day light one blue (or purple) candle and read the verse for the day.

Day 1

Today we light the first candle of Advent. This is the candle of hope. The truth is that life is hard, and sometimes we feel lost and alone. Yet we learn, slowly but surely, that having God as a friend allows us to have hope. God never leaves us. He is with us always. In fact, "God loved the people of this world so much that he gave his only Son, so that everyone who has faith in him will have eternal life and never really die" (John 3:16, CEV).

Pray together: *God, help me to get to know you more. Help me live with hope.*

Day 2

As you light the candle of hope today, read these words from the prophet Isaiah, who talked to God's people about the Light that would be coming into their dark and broken world. This light was Jesus.

> Those who walked in the dark have seen a bright light. And it shines upon everyone who lives in the land of darkest shadows. (Isaiah 9:2, CEV)

Pray together: *May I walk in the light.*

Day 3

As you light the hope candle, continue reading from Isaiah, whose words remind God's people of what God has done for them.

> Our LORD, you have made your nation stronger.

> Because of you, its people are glad and celebrate
>   like workers at harvest time
>   or like soldiers dividing up what they have taken.
> —Isaiah 9:3 (CEV)

Pray together: *May I be strong.*

Day 4

As you light the hope candle, read on in Isaiah as he offers hope to those who know God.

> You have broken the power of those who abused
> and enslaved your people.
> You have rescued them just as you saved your people
> from Midian.
> —Isaiah 9:4, (CEV)

Pray together: *Rescue me from those who want to tear me down or hurt me.*

Day 5

Light the candle of hope and hear Isaiah speak of the victory that comes from God. Think of your life and the combative situations you're facing at work or within your own family or friendships. Do you have hope that these situations will be resolved? They will, with God's help.

> The boots of marching warriors
> and the blood-stained uniforms have been fed to flames
> and eaten by fire.
> —Isaiah 9:5 (CEV)

Pray together: *May your victory be mine.*

Day 6

After you light the hope candle, listen to Isaiah prophesy of Jesus' birth, which would take place 500 or so years after he delivered his message. It was a message of hope to God's people, just as the promise of Jesus' return to earth some day gives hope to God's people in our time.

> For a child is born to us,
> a son is given to us.
> The government will rest on his shoulders.
> And he will be called:
> Wonderful Counselor, Mighty God,
> Everlasting Father, Prince of Peace.
> —Isaiah 9:6 (NLT)

Pray together: *Wonderful Counselor, Mighty God, Everlasting Father, Prince of Peace—may I also call you Friend.*

Day 7

We are at the end of the first week of Advent. As you light the candle of hope and read today's verse, think about the hope that these words can bring to those who choose God as a friend.

> His government and its peace will never end. He will rule with fairness and justice from the throne of his ancestor David for all eternity. The passionate commitment of the Lord of Heaven's Armies will make this happen! (Isaiah 9:7, NLT)

Pray together: *May I know the peace of God.*

Week Two Readings

Directions: Each day light two blue (or purple) candles and read the verse for the day.

Day 1

Today we light the second candle of Advent. This is the candle of love. One of the most famous verses in the Bible begins, "For God so loved the world that he gave his one and only Son" (John 3:16, NIV). During this next week of holiday preparations, think about how God's love crosses over from his world into ours if we let it. Listen to this whole passage about why God sent his Son to us:

> "This is how much God loved the world: He gave his Son, his one and only Son. And this is why: so that no one need be destroyed; by believing in him, anyone can have a whole and lasting life. God didn't go to all the trouble of sending his Son merely to point an accusing finger, telling the world how bad it was. He came to help, to put the world right again." (John 3:16-17, MSG)

Pray together: *God, may we accept your crazy, amazing love for us.*

Day 2

Just as Isaiah told God's people about the gift of Jesus that was coming, more than 500 years later, Jesus' cousin John had that honor too. John the Baptist started his ministry before Jesus in order to prepare the way and help people get ready to meet God's Son. Read the beginning of that adventure in the Gospel of Mark.

> This is the good news about Jesus Christ, the Son of God. It began just as God had said in the book written by Isaiah the prophet,
>
> "I am sending my messenger
>   to get the way ready for you." (Mark 1:1-2, CEV)

Pray together: *May I hear the Good News and be ready for Jesus to come to us again.*

Day 3

John was sort of an oddball. He lived alone in the wilderness. He wore animal skins and ate locusts and honey. His mission in life was to tell people about the arrival of God's Son and encourage them to change their lives, to start walking the straight and narrow path that led to a life walked with God.

> "In the desert someone is shouting,
> 'Get the road ready for the Lord!
>   Make a straight path for him.'"
> —Mark 1:3 (CEV)

Pray together: *May I make a straight path in my life.*

Day 4

A lot of people thought John was crazy. Yet a lot of other people started to listen and ask questions and listen some more. Are you listening yet?

> So John the Baptist showed up in the desert and told everyone, "Turn back to God and be baptized! Then your sins will be forgiven." (Mark 1:4, CEV)

Pray together: *May I listen to the voice of God.*

Day 5

People began to change their lives, to read God's Word, to find ways to work for God. They started to build a friendship with God. How would you describe your friendship with God?

> From all Judea and Jerusalem crowds of people went to John. They told how sorry they were for their sins, and he baptized them in the Jordan River. (Mark 1:5, CEV)

Pray together: *May I learn to be a friend of God.*

Day 6

John was talking about Jesus. He was talking to Jewish people who would have known who Isaiah was and known that he had talked about God's Son long before his birth. John wanted people to be ready to welcome God's gift of love with open arms. Are you ready?

> John also told the people, "Someone more powerful is going to come. And I am not good enough even to stoop down and untie his sandals." (Mark 1:7, CEV)

Pray together: *May I welcome God into my life.*

Day 7

John also wanted people to understand that what he was doing was a first step in getting to know Jesus. They had to take the "next step" in their friendship with God and get to know Jesus. Are you ready to take the "next step" in getting to know Jesus?

> John told them, "I baptize you with water, but he will baptize you with the Holy Spirit!" (Mark 1:8, CEV)

Pray together: *Lead me to take a "next step" in my friendship with God.*

Week Three Readings

Directions: Each day light two blue (or purple) candles and also the pink candle. Then read the reflection for the day.

Day 1

During Advent the pink or rose candle reminds us of the gift of God's Son, Jesus. It is the candle of joy. No one knew that joy better than Mary, the young teenager who was visited by the angel Gabriel and told she would be the mother of God's Son. Can you imagine receiving such news? Listen to the beginning of that amazing story.

> One month later God sent the angel Gabriel to the town of Nazareth in Galilee with a message for a virgin named Mary. She was engaged to Joseph from the family of King David. The angel greeted Mary and said, "You are truly blessed! The Lord is with you." (Luke 1:26-28, CEV)

Pray together: *May I hear your voice speak to me and call me blessed.*

Day 2

We pick up Mary's story today with her trying to figure out what was happening in her life. Listen for echoes from Isaiah when he delivered God's message of a Savior being born, hundreds of years before Jesus' birth. God's story goes back and forth across the ages, from generation to generation. It's a story for all of God's people, from the beginning of time to its end. It's a story for you.

> Mary was confused by the angel's words and wondered what they meant. Then the angel told Mary, "Don't be afraid! God is pleased with you, and you will have a son. His name will be Jesus. He will be great and will be called the Son of God Most High. The Lord God will make him king, as his ancestor David was. He will rule the people of Israel forever, and his kingdom will never end." (Luke 1:29-33, CEV)

Pray together: *May I not be afraid to invite God into my life.*

Day 3

Sometimes, though, God's Word makes us ask questions. We don't always get it, which was certainly true in Mary's case.

> Mary asked the angel, "How can this happen? I am not married!"
>
> The angel answered, 'The Holy Spirit will come down to you, and God's power will come over you. So your child will be called the holy Son of God. Your relative Elizabeth is also going to have a son, even though she is old. No one thought she could ever have a baby, but in three months she will have a son. Nothing is impossible for God!" (Luke 1:34-37, CEV)

Pray together: *May I trust that God makes all things possible.*

Day 4

So Mary knew nothing was impossible for God, and she was filled with great joy at the gift God was giving her, as unbelievable as it seemed. Her response is simple. She didn't hesitate and hem and haw over whether to accept God's plan. She didn't gush over the enormity of the responsibility. She only said,

> "I am the Lord's servant! Let it happen as you have said." And the angel left her. (Luke 1:38, CEV)

Pray together: *May I live life in ways that follow God's plans for me.*

Day 5

Soon after Gabriel's visit, Mary went to see her cousin Elizabeth, whose pregnancy Gabriel had told Mary about. After Elizabeth greeted and blessed Mary, Mary was so overcome with joy that she sang a song of praise to God that we call the Magnificat. Mary was basically telling God, "You are magnificent!" Hear her song:

> With all my heart I praise the Lord,
>   and I am glad because of God my Savior.
> God cares for me, his humble servant.
> From now on, all people will say
>   God has blessed me.
> God All-Powerful has done great things for me,
>   and his name is holy.
> —Luke 1:46-49 (CEV)

Pray together: God, may I hear your heavenly song and be moved to praise you like Mary.

Day 6

And Mary continued with her song of praise:

> He always shows mercy
>   to everyone who worships him.
> The Lord has used his powerful arm
>   to scatter those who are proud.
> God drags strong rulers from their thrones
>   and puts humble people in places of power.
> God gives the hungry good things to eat,
> and sends the rich away
>   with nothing.
> He helps his servant Israel
>   and is always merciful to his people.
> —Luke 1:50-54 (CEV)

Pray together: *May I know your mercy in my life.*

Day 7

Mary found joy in her friendship with God, even in the midst of what most people would find to be an earth-shaking, life-changing event. Even better, she knew that this joy had crossed over the ages, all part of the promise that God made to Abraham back in Old Testament times that his descendants would be as numerous as the grains of sand in the desert or stars in the sky.

> Mary concluded her song with this declaration:

> "The Lord made this promise to our ancestors, to Abraham and his family forever!" (Luke 1:55, CEV).

Pray together: *Lord, help me sing "Joy to the World" and glorify your name this Christmas.*

Week Four Readings

Directions: Each day light all four candles, and then read the reflection for the day.

Day 1

The fourth Advent candle is the candle of peace. It helps us remember the gift that fills our lives when we trust Jesus. God and his plans are so much bigger than we can ever imagine or understand. He reminds us of that in Isaiah 55:8 when he says, "My thoughts and my ways are not like yours" (CEV). Yet the peace that God can bring into our messy human lives is a peace like no other. Take it from Mary, mother of Jesus. She had quite the wild ride with God. Listen as the Christmas story unfolds.

> About that time Emperor Augustus gave orders for the names of all the people to be listed in record books. These first records were made when Quirinius was governor of Syria. Everyone had to go to their own hometown to be listed. So Joseph had to leave Nazareth in Galilee and go to Bethlehem in Judea. Long ago Bethlehem had been King David's hometown, and Joseph went there because he was from David's family. (Luke 2:1-4, CEV)

Can you imagine being Mary? Almost ready to give birth and having to make a long, hard trip . . . trusting God had everything under control.

Pray together: *Lord, help me trust that you've got my life under control.*

Day 2

People turning away God's gift of love is not a new thing. Don't you wonder what those who turned Mary and Joseph away thought in hindsight?

> Mary was engaged to Joseph and traveled with him to Bethlehem. She was soon going to have a baby, and while they were there, she gave birth to her first-born son. She dressed him in baby clothes and laid him on a bed of hay, because there was no room for them in the inn. (Luke 2:5-7, CEV)

Pray together: *God, may I have eyes that see you even in the smallest, humblest of places.*

Day 3

And then there were the shepherds, everyday working guys, later the perpetual catch-all characters of church Christmas pageants. Yet they had an experience that not many people have—angels showing up at their workplace and delivering a memo that forever changed their lives.

> That night in the fields near Bethlehem some shepherds were guarding their sheep. All at once an angel came down to them from the Lord, and the brightness of the Lord's glory flashed around them. The shepherds were frightened. But the angel said, 'Don't be afraid! I have good news for you, which will make everyone happy. This very day in King David's hometown a Savior was born for you. He is Christ the Lord. You will know who he is, because you will find him dressed in baby clothes and lying on a bed of hay. (Luke 2:8-12, CEV)

Pray together: *God, may I hear the Good News and have no fear.*

Day 4

Then came the message of peace. Isaiah had told God's people about the one who was coming, the Son of God who would be the Wonderful Counselor, Mighty God, Everlasting Father, and Prince of Peace. Jesus, born as a baby, would become a king who would usher in a reign of peace on behalf of all people.

> Suddenly many other angels came down from heaven and joined in praising God. They said: "Praise God in heaven! Peace on earth to everyone who pleases God." (Luke 2:13-14, CEV)

Pray together: *May I become part of your peace process, God.*

Day 5

This message of peace on earth and goodwill to all was too wonderful to keep to themselves, so the shepherds set off to find this infant king. Have you ever had a piece of good news that you just had to share with someone? With a lot of someones? Did you ever want to shout it from the rooftops? That's how the shepherds felt that first Christmas.

> After the angels had left and gone back to heaven, the shepherds said to each other, "Let's go to Bethlehem and see what the Lord has told us about." They hurried off and found Mary and Joseph, and they saw the baby lying on a bed of hay. (Luke 2:15-16, CEV)

Pray together: *God, may I see the good you put in my life, no matter how small.*

Day 6

Imagine being Mary. First the angel appears to you and says you will be the mother of God's Son. Then you find yourself pregnant and nine months later delivering the King of the universe in a barn surrounded by donkeys and goats. Then a handful of smelly shepherds show up and tell you they were visited by the angels, too, who told them about your new little family. Panic or peace? What do you think Mary was feeling? What would you have been feeling?

> When the shepherds saw Jesus, they told his parents what the angel had said about him. Everyone listened and was surprised. But Mary kept thinking about all this and wondering what it meant. (Luke 2:17-19, CEV)

Pray together: *May I think about your words, God, and wonder how they might guide my life.*

Day 7

The shepherds didn't stay long. They had to get back to their flocks. But they didn't stop talking about what they had witnessed.

> As the shepherds returned to their sheep, they were praising God and saying wonderful things about him. Everything they had seen and heard was just as the angel had said. (Luke 2:20, CEV)

Pray together: *Lord, help me accept your gift of love that remains the same from generation to generation. Lord, I praise your holy name.*

Family History Facts

Directions: Interview people to find answers to the following questions. Be sure to bring this fact sheet with you to dinner, as you'll continue to interview during your meal. (You don't have to write during dinner, though; just listen and eat!)

1. Who is the oldest person in your extended family?

2. Who has all four grandparents living?

3. Who had a family member live to be over 95? What was his/her name?

4. In what state(s) does your family live? Who lives farthest away? Who lives closest?

5. What countries did your (great-) grandparents come from? Have you ever visited those places? If yes, where and when?

6. Which relative of yours tells the funniest stories?

7. Which relative of yours tells the longest stories?

8. What church/churches does your family and/or extended family attend?

9. Who is one person in your family/extended family whose faith you admire? Why?

10. If you have extra time during fellowship, tell a funny story or favorite memory involving one of your relatives.

Jesse Tree Stories and Symbol Suggestions

Person/People	Bible Verses	Suggested Symbol
1. Adam and Eve	Genesis 2	apple or garden
2. Abraham and Sarah	Genesis 15:1-6; 22:1-19	stars in the sky
3. Isaac and Rebekah	Genesis 24; 25:19-26	water well or twin babies
4. Jacob and Leah	Genesis 28:10-17; 29:15-35	ladder
5. Judah and Tamar	Genesis 38:24-30; Matthew 1:3	staff and cord
6. Salmon and Rahab	Joshua 2:8-14; Matthew 1:5	red cord hanging from window
7. Boaz and Ruth	Ruth 4:7-22	sheaves of grain
8. David and Bathsheba	1 Samuel 16:1-13; 1 Kings 1:11-31	horn of oil or shepherd's crook
9. Solomon and Naamah	1 Kings 3:1-15; 4:29–5:5; 14:21,31	crown
10. Mary	Luke 1:26-38,46-55	heart
11. Joseph	Matthew 1:19-25	carpenter's tools
12. Jesus	Luke 2:1-20; John 1:1-19	candle, manger

Note: If you have enough participants to work on additional people and symbols, cut out three 6" birds representing the three prophets who spoke of the coming Messiah—Samuel, Isaiah, and John the Baptist.

Person/People	Bible Verses	Suggested Symbol
13. Samuel	1 Samuel 3–4:1; 16:1-13	sleeping boy or speech bubble with the words "Here I am!"
14. Isaiah	Isaiah 6; 9:2-7; 11:1-5	lips
15. John the Baptist	Isaiah 40:1-5; Matthew 3:1-12	flowing river

Carol History Trivia

Match each statement to its correct answer below. Feel free to join up with another group for shared brain power.

1. Originally I was the name of a circle dance used by Celtic Europe for pagan harvest celebrations. Later St. Francis of Assisi used the musical structure of my tunes and catchy rhythms to create *laudas*, which eventually became the basis for the Christmas songs we sing today.

2. I started out life as a slave song about freedom.

3. My words were set to music by a famous Jewish composer who only wanted his music used for nonreligious purposes.

4. I am the first well-known, often sung Christmas carol written in the United States. I was written by a Unitarian minister in Massachusetts in 1849.

5. I am the oldest Christmas carol known in North America, written by a missionary to the Indians in Quebec in 1648.

6. I am the oldest-known Christmas carol to have kept my original words used in the nineteenth-century Latin version, called *O Antiphons*.

7. I brought Christmas carols back into Christmas Eve worship in 1223.

8. This religious group banned Christmas carols, and for a while banned Christmas celebrations in the colonies and in England.

9. I was written by a French businessman/poet who later left the church, my music was composed by a Jewish musician, and I was banned for many years because of both of those facts.

10. I was written as a poem in response to the horrors of the Civil War and the assassination of President Lincoln. The church organist set me to music, and I was first performed by the church's children's choir in 1868.

11. My music and words have survived intact for almost three hundred years, making me one of the most well-known carols to stay the same over a long period of time.

12. My words are the author's interpretation of Psalm 98:4-9, and he did not intend for me to be a Christmas carol. In fact, I was originally written in 1719 when Christmas carols were not often sung.

13. I was written by a woman in 1941. Almost twenty years later, I became an overnight hit when played on the radio with a slightly different name and different writers credited. My composer later received her proper recognition, and I became a much-loved TV Christmas special, first appearing in 1968.

14. I was written in 1816, set to a guitar accompaniment in 1818, and have become the most recorded/performed/sung carol in history.

Trivia Answer Choices

a. "Silent Night"

b. carol

c. "O Little Town of Bethlehem"

d. "O Come, All Ye Faithful"

e. "Carol of the Drum"

f. "Joy to the World"

g. "Hark! the Herald Angels Sing"

h. "O Come, O Come, Emmanuel"

i. "The Huron Carol" or "'Twas in the Moon of Wintertime"

j. "O Holy Night"

k. "Go Tell It on the Mountain"

l. "It Came upon the Midnight Clear"

m. Francis of Assisi

n. The Puritans

Christmas around the World

Directions: Working together with other individuals or families, try to match each country name to its correct lettered display.

A. _____

B. _____

C. _____

D. _____

E. _____

F. _____

G. _____

H. _____

Country Names

India   Romania

Venezuela   China

Ethiopia   Egypt

Greece   Iraq

Spend Less–Gift Refocusing Worksheet

God so loved this world that he sent his only Son to us. To us! That gift was so generous and so perfect that sometimes we continue to think Christmas is all about us. Yet when God shared the gift of his Son with us, an inward focus wasn't what he was dreaming of. God wants to see us fully accepting his gift of love by turning our Christmas focus outward and sharing that love with others. Challenge yourself this Christmas to spend less on stuff and give more of yourself back to God's kingdom work. Edit these worksheet categories as needed to reflect your typical Christmas giving, estimating the average total amounts that are spent for each person or category. Then follow the steps below to reduce your budget and shift your resources and your gift-giving focus.

Child 1 $ _____

Child 2 $ _____

Child 3 $ _____

Child 4 $ _____

Child 5 $ _____

Child 6 $ _____

Spouse (x2) $ _____

His Parents $ _____

Her Parents $ _____

Extended Family $ _____

Teacher(s) $ _____

Service Workers $ _____ (bus driver, mail carrier, stylist, etc.)

Coworkers $ _____

Friends $ _____

Holiday Meals $ _____

Holiday Baking $ _____

Miscellaneous $ _____

TOTAL $ _____

10% of TOTAL = _____ (subtract this number from TOTAL)

NEW SPEND LESS TOTAL $ _____

10% of new TOTAL $ _____ (donation to Advent Conspiracy or mission project)

$ _____ (subtract donation from SPEND LESS TOTAL)

FINAL SPEND LESS TOTAL $ _____

My goal this year is to SPEND LESS than $_____ and give $_____ to Living Water International or the church-chosen mission project of _____.

For use with chapter 15, "A Service "Advent"ure," in 'Tis the Season: Church Celebrations for Advent & Christmas by Rachel Gilmore © 2011 by Judson Press, Valley Forge, PA. All rights reserved. www.judsonpress.com.

Directions: Complete necessary information for front side of postcard. Copy or print your postcard on heavy-weight cardstock.

front side

[Name of your church]

*invites you to our house for
Christmas this year!*

Name of program / Month / Day / Time

(optional: followed by refreshments)
(optional: Infant/Toddler nurseries will be provided)

(optional: insert here your church's Christmas Eve service schedule)
(optional: Infant/Toddler nurseries will be provided)

(optional: insert here your church's weekly worship schedule)
(optional: Come as you are. Just bring yourself. No need to RSVP.)

[church address / website / phone / e-mail]

back side

insert a Christmas graphic / clip art of your choice

choose a Bible verse that relates to your program

(optional: personal message from the church, e.g.,
We wish you a Merry Christmas and hope to see you at our house soon.
—Your friends at [name of your church])

For use with chapter 15, "A Service "Advent"ure," in *'Tis the Season: Church Celebrations for Advent & Christmas* by Rachel Gilmore © 2011 by Judson Press, Valley Forge, PA. All rights reserved. www.judsonpress.com.

Twelve Days of Christmas Symbols and Scripture List

(handout for game show host)

A partridge in a pear tree / Jesus / Matthew 23:37

Two turtledoves / Old and New Testament / 2 Timothy 3:14-17

Three French hens / faith, hope, and love / 1 Corinthians 13:13

Four calling birds / four Gospels / John 21:24-25

Five gold rings / Pentateuch or Book of the Law / Psalm 119:1-2

Six geese a-laying / six days of Creation / Genesis 1

Seven swans a-swimming / seven gifts of the Holy Spirit / Romans 12:6-8 (*Note:* The host may need to help teams with this one by saying something like "Seven gifts of the——" or "Seven gifts of the H—— S——.")

Eight maids a-milking / eight Beatitudes / Matthew 5:3-10 (*Note:* The host may need to provide a hint, such as "These were part of Jesus' most famous sermon" or "Jesus proclaimed these famous sayings as part of the Sermon on the Mount.")

Nine ladies dancing / nine fruit of the Spirit / Galatians 5:22-23

Ten lords a-leaping / Ten Commandments / Exodus 20:1-17

Eleven pipers piping / eleven faithful disciples / Acts 1:13

Twelve drummers drumming / twelve points in the Apostles' Creed / Romans 10:9

Day 1 bonus: What does the pear tree symbolize? (the cross)

Day 2 bonus: How many books are in the Old and New Testament together? (66)

Day 3 bonus: What does the Bible say is the greatest of these 3 gifts? (love)

Day 4 bonus: Name one or more of the four Gospels included in the New Testament. (Matthew, Mark, Luke, John)

Day 5 bonus: Name one or more of the books of the Pentateuch. Hint: They are the first five books of the Hebrew Bible, our Old Testament. (Genesis, Exodus, Leviticus, Numbers, Deuteronomy)

Day 6 bonus: What did the Lord create on each day of creation? (day/night, water/sky, earth/plants, sun/moon, birds/sea creatures, animals, people)

Day 7 bonus: Before reading the Scriptures, name one or more of the gifts of the Spirit. Earn one point per gift. ([1] prophecy, [2] ministry, [3] teaching, [4] exhortation, [5] giving, [6] leading, and [7] compassion)

Day 8 bonus: Before reading the Scripture, name one or more of the Beatitudes. Earn one point per correct answer. (Blessed are: [1] the poor in spirit, [2] those who mourn, [3] the meek, [4] those who hunger and thirst for righteousness, [5] the merciful, [6] the pure in heart, [7] the peacemakers, [8] those who are persecuted for righteousness' sake.)

Day 9 bonus: Before reading the Scripture, name one or more of the fruit of the Spirit. Earn one point for each correct answer. ([1] love, [2] joy, [3] peace, [4] patience, [5] kindness, [6] goodness, [7] faithfulness, [8] gentleness, and [9] self-control)

Day 10 bonus: Before reading the Scripture, name one or more of the commandments. Earn one point for each correct answer. ([1] You shall have no other gods before me. [2] Do not make an idol. [3] Do not take God's name in vain. [4] Remember the Sabbath day. [5] Honor your father and mother. [6] Do not murder. [7] Do not commit adultery. [8] Do not steal. [9] Do not bear false witness. [10] Do not covet.)

Day 11 bonus: Before reading the Scripture, name one or more of the Eleven. Earn one point for each correct name. ([1] Simon Peter, [2] Andrew, [3] James, [4] John, [5] Philip, [6] Bartholomew, [7] Matthew, [8] Thomas, [9] James bar [son of] Alphaeus, [10] Simon the Zealot, [11] Judas bar [son of] James [or Thaddeus; see Matthew 10:1-4; Mark 3:16-19])

Day 12 bonus: Earn extra points by reciting some or all of the points (phrases) in the Creed. ([1] I believe in God, the Father almighty, creator of heaven and earth. [2] I believe in Jesus Christ, his only Son, our Lord. [3] He was conceived by the power of the Holy Spirit and born of the virgin Mary. [4] He suffered under Pontius Pilate, was crucified, died, and was buried. He descended into hell [the grave] (omit or substitute if your religious traditions dictates). [5] On the third day he rose again. He ascended into heaven, and is seated at the right hand of the Father. [6] He will come again to judge the living and the dead. [7] I believe in the Holy Spirit, [8] the holy catholic church, [9] the communion of saints, [10] the forgiveness of sins, [11] the resurrection of the body, [12] and life everlasting.)

Invite the group to recite the creed together—or listen as the host reads it aloud. (*Note:* If your group isn't familiar with the Apostles' Creed or opposes the use of creeds, the pastor might be able to explain the pros and cons. Basically, the creeds [e.g., Apostles', Nicene, and others] emerged during early church history when Christians were still developing their identity and needing to put into writing the fundamental beliefs that were worth dying for—because people were, indeed, dying for their new faith. The creeds also served as judicial rulings that excluded certain early beliefs as heretical [even though many persist in one form or another, even today!]).

For use with chapter 17, "The Twelve Days of Christmas and the Never-Ending Story," in *'Tis the Season: Church Celebrations for Advent & Christmas* by Rachel Gilmore © 2011 by Judson Press, Valley Forge, PA. All rights reserved. www.judsonpress.com.

Twelve Days of Christmas Cartons

Directions

1. Gather one egg carton and one set of plastic eggs per household or child participant.

2. Get 12 slips of 4.25" x 3.6" paper, collect one of each of the Bible verse stickers and put one verse on each slip of paper.

3. Look at the clip art and/or sticker pictures of the 12 song items. Decide if you will use this preprinted art for your eggs or if you will draw your own. Make sure each slip of paper has its Bible verse sticker and some kind of artwork showing the object in the song that goes with that verse. If you want, add a picture of the Christian symbolism that you learned about tonight.

4. Roll up each piece of paper and put one verse in each egg.

5. Using the permanent markers and assorted decorating supplies, decorate the eggs with their matching number from the song (e.g., #2 for the egg with two turtledoves) or any other design. If using permanent marker, let each color dry briefly before handling.

6 Decorate the egg carton by covering it in Christmas paper.

7. Each day from December 26 to January 6, open one egg and read the Bible verse.

For use with chapter 17, "The Twelve Days of Christmas and the Never-Ending Story," in *'Tis the Season: Church Celebrations for Advent & Christmas* by Rachel Gilmore © 2011 by Judson Press, Valley Forge, PA. All rights reserved. www.judsonpress.com.